31472400277707

CARSON CITY LIBRARY
900 North Roop Street
Carson City, NV 89701
775-887-2244
WITHDRAWN
NOV 29 2016

the unbeatable Squirrel Girl

COLLECTION EDITOR: **JENNIFER GRÜNWALD**
ASSOCIATE EDITOR: **SARAH BRUNSTAD**
EDITOR, SPECIAL PROJECTS: **MARK D. BEAZLEY**
VP, PRODUCTION & SPECIAL PROJECTS: **JEFF YOUNGQUIST**
SVP PRINT, SALES & MARKETING: **DAVID GABRIEL**
BOOK DESIGNER: **JAY BOWEN**

EDITOR IN CHIEF: **AXEL ALONSO**
CHIEF CREATIVE OFFICER: **JOE QUESADA**
PUBLISHER: **DAN BUCKLEY**
EXECUTIVE PRODUCER: **ALAN FINE**

THE UNBEATABLE SQUIRREL GIRL VOL. 1. Contains material originally published in magazine form as THE UNBEATABLE SQUIRREL GIRL #1-8, MARVEL SUPER-HEROES #8, GLX-MAS SPECIAL #1, THE THING #8 and AGE OF HEROES #3. First printing 2016. ISBN# 978-1-302-90224-7. Published by MARVEL WORLDWIDE, INC., a subsidiary of MARVEL ENTERTAINMENT, LLC. OFFICE OF PUBLICATION: 135 West 50th Street, New York, NY 10020. Copyright © 2016 MARVEL No similarity between any of the names, characters, persons, and/or institutions in this magazine with those of any living or dead person or institution is intended, and any such similarity which may exist is purely coincidental. **Printed in China.** ALAN FINE, President, Marvel Entertainment; DAN BUCKLEY, President, TV, Publishing & Brand Management; JOE QUESADA, Chief Creative Officer; TOM BREVOORT, SVP of Publishing; DAVID BOGART, SVP of Business Affairs & Operations, Publishing & Partnership; C.B. CEBULSKI, VP of Brand Management & Development, Asia; DAVID GABRIEL, SVP of Sales & Marketing, Publishing; JEFF YOUNGQUIST, VP of Production & Special Projects; DAN CARR, Executive Director of Publishing Technology; ALEX MORALES, Director of Publishing Operations; SUSAN CRESPI, Production Manager; STAN LEE, Chairman Emeritus. For information regarding advertising in Marvel Comics or on Marvel.com, please contact Vit DeBellis, Integrated Sales Manager, at vdebellis@marvel.com. For Marvel subscription inquiries, please call 888-511-5480. **Manufactured between 6/24/2016 and 9/12/2016 by R.R. DONNELLEY ASIA PRINTING SOLUTIONS, CHINA.**

10 9 8 7 6 5 4 3 2 1

the unbeatable Squirrel Girl

Ryan North
WRITER

Erica Henderson
ARTIST

Maris Wicks *(#1)*, **Kyle Starks** *(#3)*,
Chris Giarrusso *(#4)* & **Eloise Narrington** *(#5-6)*
TRADING CARD ART

Rico Renzi
COLOR ARTIST

VC's Clayton Cowles
LETTERER

Erica Henderson
COVER ART

Jon Moisan & Jake Thomas
ASSISTANT EDITORS

Wil Moss
EDITOR

Tom Brevoort
EXECUTIVE EDITOR

SPECIAL THANKS TO LISSA PATILLO

Marvel Super-Heroes #8

PLOT/ARTIST: **STEVE DITKO**
SCRIPT: **WILL MURRAY**
COLORIST: **CHRISTIE SCHEELE**
LETTERER: **BRAD K. JOYCE**
COVER ART: **ERIK LARSEN**

GLX-Mas Special #1 "EGGNOG, TOILET PAPER, AND PEACE ON EARTH"

WRITER: **DAN SLOTT** ARTIST: **MATT HALEY**
LETTERER: **DAVE LANPHEAR**
COVER ART: **PAUL PELLETIER, RICK MAGYAR & WIL QUINTANA**
ASSISTANT EDITORS: **ANDY SCHMIDT, MOLLY LAZER** & **AUBREY SITTERSON**
EDITOR: **TOM BREVOORT**

The Thing #8 "LAST HAND"

WRITER: **DAN SLOTT** ARTIST: **KIERON DWYER**
COLOR ARTIST: **LAURA VILLARI**
LETTERER: **DAVE LANPHEAR**
COVER ART: **ANDREA DI VITO & LAURA VILLARI**
ASSISTANT EDITORS: **ANDY SCHMIDT, MOLLY LAZER** & **AUBREY SITTERSON**
EDITOR: **TOM BREVOORT**

Age of Heroes #3 "NUTS TO THIS"

WRITER: **DAN SLOTT** ARTIST: **TY TEMPLETON**
COLOR ARTIST: **JORGE MAESE**
LETTERER: **DAVE LANPHEAR**
COVER ART: **YANICK PAQUETTE, MICHEL LACOMBE** & **NATHAN FAIRBAIRN**
EDITORS: **LAUREN SANKOVITCH & TOM BREVOORT**

1

Squirrel Girl, Squirrel Girl! She's a human and also squirrel!
Can she climb up a tree? Yes she can, easily.
That's whyyyy
Her name is Squirrel Girl!
Hey, mister! Give us your purse!
Is she tough? Listen bud:
It's not a purse! It's a leather satchel.
She's got partially squirrel blood.
Who's her friend? Don't you know:
That's the squirrel, Tippy-Toe.
Huh? Is she singing?
Is that--is that a tail?
Surprise! She likes to talk to squirrels!
OW!
KA-POW
GAH!

You now have the Spider-Man theme song stuck in your head for the rest of this issue. *You're welcome.*

Wait, did I say the Spider-Man theme song? *Obviously* I meant the ***Squirrel Girl*** theme song. Who even *is* Spider-Man?

NOT PICTURED: Other tiny boxes labelled "Ant-Man's Tiny Vans," "Ant-Man's Aunt's Flans," and "Ant-Man's Rejected Costumes (OFF-Brand)"

There's more to being a super hero than just being the strongest! For example, you might also be the fastest, or the smartest, or have the ability to breathe in space like it isn't even a big deal.

Also, my name rhymes. Yes, that too is but one of the *several* ways in which I am totally regular.

I'm, uh, just moving all these empty boxes into my dorm, and that way I'll be ready to help when it's time to move out of the dorms!

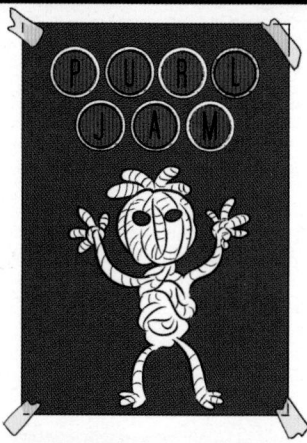

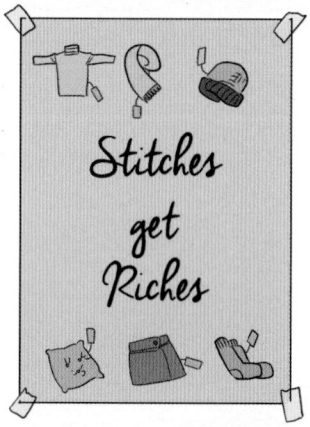

DID YOU KNOW: Mew is named after "Mewnir," which is the name of Cat Thor's hammer? DID YOU ALSO KNOW: Cat Thor is a character in Nancy's Fan Fiction, "Cat Thor: Cat God of Cat Thunder"??

DID YOU KNOW: college administrator was the job Kraven the Hunter was training for before he took a chance weekend safari getaway? Yes! It's almost possibly a fact!

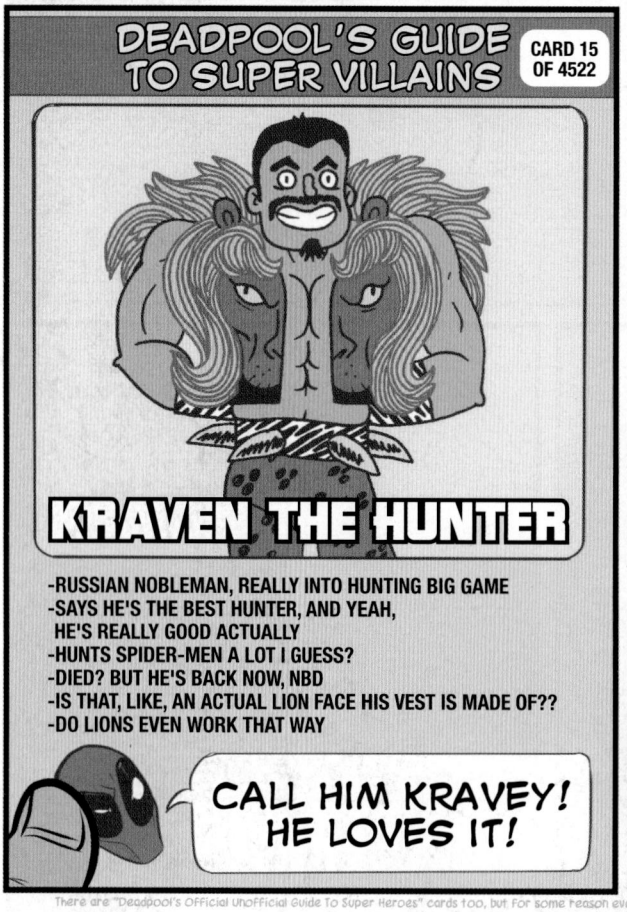

There are "Deadpool's Official Unofficial Guide To Super Heroes" cards too, but for some reason every pack is like 99% pictures of Deadpool looking at himself in a mirror and giving himself a thumbs up.

Listen, all I have are these "Deadpool Super Villain" cards, not "Deadpool Great One-Liners For Heroes To Use On Super Villain" cards. I'm not made of money over here.

In retrospect, the song *does* spend a surprisingly large percentage of its time describing my friends, my favourite foods, and where I like to hang out. Hindsight's always 20/20, huh?

Congratulations to "LET'S GET NUTS" for beating out runners-up "LET'S GET CRAZY" and "LET'S BECOME ECCENTRIC" in the What Should Squirrel Girl Say When Biting Her Way Out Of A Net Competition, 2015

Another runner-up was "LET'S GO BANANAS," before that phrase was disqualified for also having competed in the What Should Man-Ape Say When Biting Into A Banana Really Intensely Competition, 2015.

Squirrels in pants? Squirrels... *eating* pants? *Squirrels secretly replacing pants with other squirrels??*

And don't say it's because it's on his Deadpool trading card because those are *non-canon.*

If you *think* there's someone who goes here and who looks like me then my only comment on that matter is *"Okay wow she sounds hot!"*

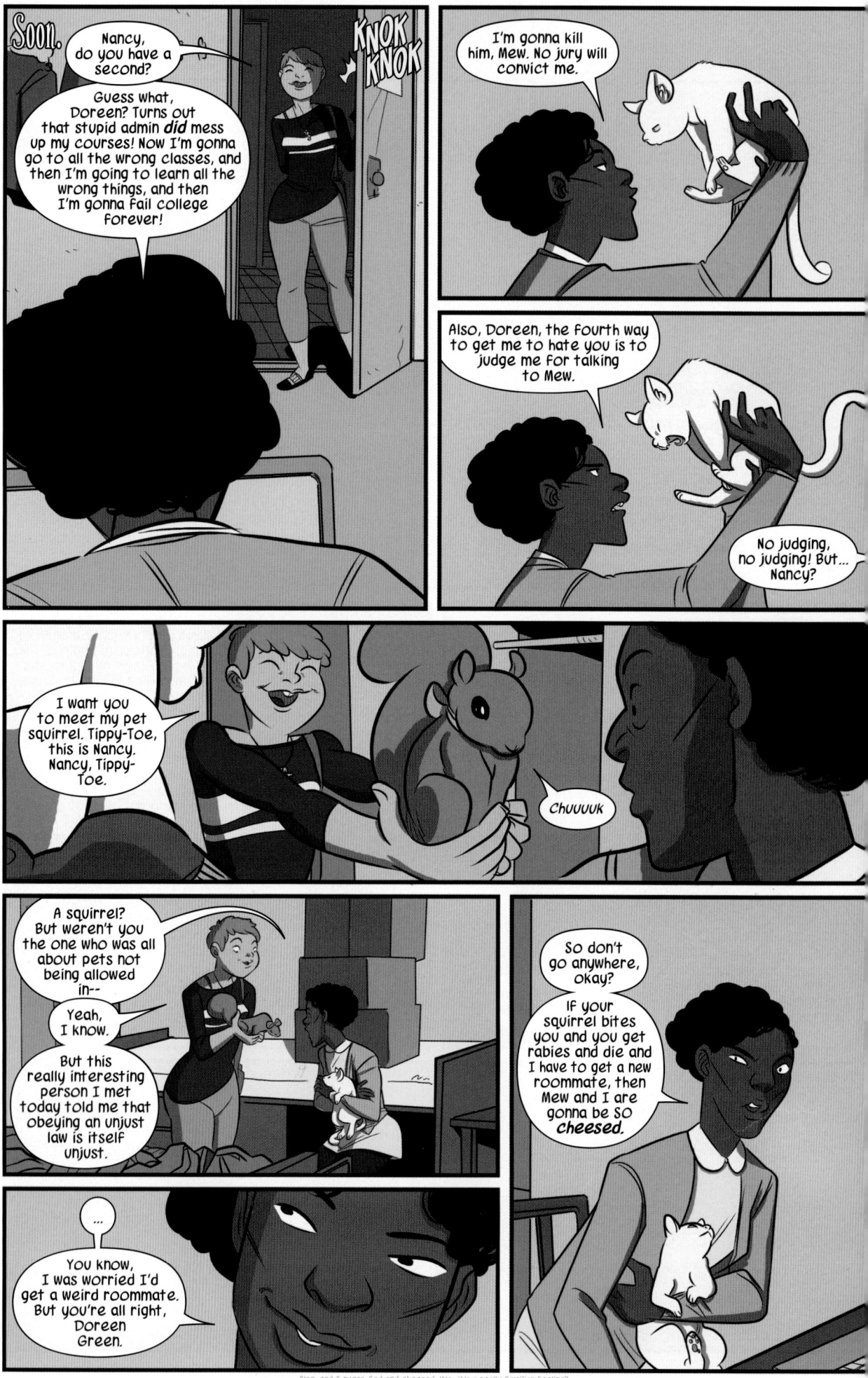

Also, sad I guess. Sad and cheesed. It's--it's a really familiar feeling?

Those of you who *can* speak Northeastern variant Squirrelese are freaking out right now, but don't tell anyone! Keep it a surprise for the rest of us who have to read the next page to find out what the deal is, okay?

Nancy, would you excuse us for a moment?

Come on, Tippy. I'm pretty sure the entire planet isn't totally doomed.
It is! Something colossal is headed towards Earth, Doreen! The Squirrel Information Network has reports from squirrels around the world of stars being blocked out!

Calm down. Hey, since when do squirrels stargaze? And from where?
Forest observatories, obviously.
Guess there's still some stuff you have left to learn about squirrels after all, huh?

Seriously though, Doreen: whatever it is, it's colossal and it's headed here and it's not stopping. It's up to us to save the planet!
How much time have we got?
I dunno. I mean, it's millions and millions of miles out in space, so you know: definitely a while. Still!

Well, what are you worried about then, you big baby? Space is huge and we've got plenty of time to figure this out. Come on, let's go to orientation. After all...
...what's the worst that could happen?

Coming next issue...
...the worst that could happen!

Letters From Nuts

Ryan!

Erica!

Send letters to mheroes@marvel.com or 135 W 50th St, 7th Floor, New York, NY 10020 (Please mark "OKAY TO PRINT")

Hello! We're Erica and Ryan and Rico, we're writing and drawing and coloring a comic about a woman with squirrel powers. We've actually been writing and drawing and coloring this comic for YEARS, decades really, and last month Marvel came to us and asked if they could publish it, and we said "YES!" and then went on to say "Also we've been kinda using your character so you don't really have to ask, also thanks for not suing us."

OKAY NO that's nut true. We only started this comic recently! But we ARE following in the footsteps of the people who have made Squirrel Girl comics before: great guys like Will Murray, Steve Ditko, Dan Slott, Paul Pelletier, Brian Michael Bendis and Mike Deodato!

This book is an experiment: can a book like this find an audience? Will people TRULY read a comic about someone who dresses up like a rodent-like animal and fights crime in a major metropolitan area, even if that animal ISN'T a bat?? We hope they will. If you liked this comic, share it! Tell your friends! Tell the WHOLE WORLD you liked it, because then they might like it too, and then we'll all get more comics like this: fun, funny, awesome books about a crime-fighter with a utility belt and animal-themed gadgets (again, NOT a bat). And if you've got a computer, you can check out unbeatablesquirrelgirl.tumblr.com where we post SNEAK PEEKS at upcoming issues and behind-the-scenes art!

We thought we'd start here with your letters. You can send them to MHEROES@MARVEL.COM, and don't forget to mark them "OKAY TO PRINT" so we know your letter is cool to print. But since this is our first issue all we've gotten so far are some TOTALLY FAKE LETTERS we'll use to get the ball rolling! Can YOU send us something better? I'd sincerely like to see that!!

Q: Excuse me, but how are you following me, how are you getting all this information??

- D. Green

A: Erica is really good at sketching quickly AND at being discreet. A winning combination!

Q: Who wrote Squirrel Girl's theme song?

- Pat W.

A: The song was composed by Academy Award winner Paul Francis Webster and Robert "Bob" Harris in 1967, but at the time it was accidentally applied to another obscure Marvel character named "Spider-Man." Several decades later we detected this error and corrected it, restoring the song to its originally intended glory, and now it's totally about a woman who talks to squirrels.

Q: Who would win in a fight, Squirrel Girl or the Hulk?

- Jenn K.

A: If you ask the Hulk team, they might say something different, which is frankly ADORABLE, but clearly it's Squirrel Girl. Is their character called "The Unbeatable Hulk"? No, they call him "The Incredible Hulk," as in "Incredible! The Hulk just got beat up by Squirrel Girl, she's the greatest and I love her forever!!"

Q: Who would win in a fight, Squirrel Girl or Ms. Marvel?

- Emily H.

A: Yo, why are they fighting? Doreen and Kamala are on the same side here, so it's LITERALLY CRAZY that they're fighting. A better question is who would Squirrel Girl and Ms. Marvel fight FIRST?? My money is on EVERYONE WHO STANDS IN THEIR WAY.

Q: Who would win in a fight, Tippy-Toe the Squirrel or Howard the Duck?

- Chip Z.

A: Tippy-Toe is a regular squirrel with zero super powers, and Howard the Duck is a sentient duck who is approximately as smart as the average human! That said, Tippy-Toe. PROVE ME WRONG, HOWARD.

Q: Who would YOU rather fight, one squirrel-sized Hulk or a hundred Hulk-sized squirrels?

- Lucy W.

A: Doreen would obviously take the squirrel-sized Hulk, seeing as she'd never want to fight squirrels since they are ULTIMATE PALS. Personally, I'd take the squirrel-sized Hulk too, because while I wouldn't like the Hulk when he's angry, I would LOVE him when ADORABLY-SIZED, super-cute, and could fit inside a bottle of pop.

I don't know why I apparently keep trying to pick a fight with the Hulk team here. Send us some letters! DO IT!!

Thanks everyone, and we'll see you next month!

When you see this: AR, open up the MARVEL AR APP (available on applicable Apple ® iOS or Android ™ devices) and use your camera-enabled device to unlock extra-special exclusive features!

2
EH!

Should we say you'll find him deep within the...interGALACTUS stellar medium?? We shouldn't? Oh. Okay.

The next five rules of Mew Club are to tell everyone about Mew Club; we need members really badly

Not pictured: Way Too Lazy To Set Up A Booth Club

Hey, did you know you can give yourself tattoos at home? It's true! ***But don't tell any authority figures I told you,*** I don't want to get in trouble

Here we are in issue 2 already summarizing what happened in issue 1! It's fine for now, but at a certain point I'm gonna have to stop these summaries and you'll just have to buy the comics to find out what happened, okay??

I believe the canonical attractiveness hierarchy runs--when going from most to least hunky--from hyperhunk, to megahunk, to hunk, to minihunk, and, finally, to nanohunk.

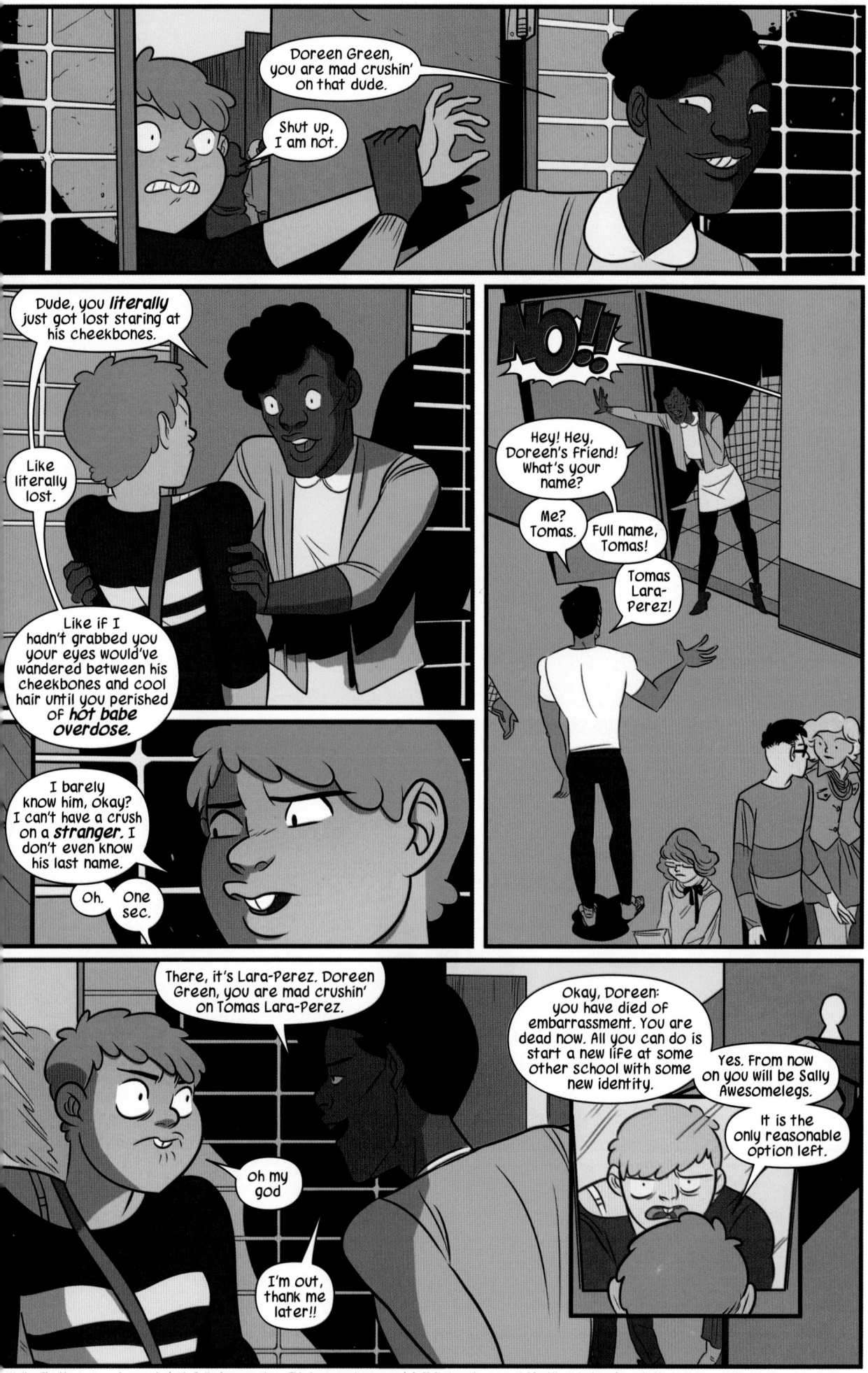

Hello, I'm the new exchange student, Sally Awesomelegs. This is my real name and definitely not a secret identity I just made up in the bathroom while looking at my legs.

Yes, Tippy-Toe did absolutely start this page imagining that window would dramatically smash around her as she leapt through it.

Honestly I wish there was time to do both, but there's not, and a girl has to make choices sometimes. Someone else join anime club for me, I'll catch up later.

People who make fun of selfies always act like they wouldn't take a selfie after they defeated Galactus. People who make fun of selfies are *dang liars.*

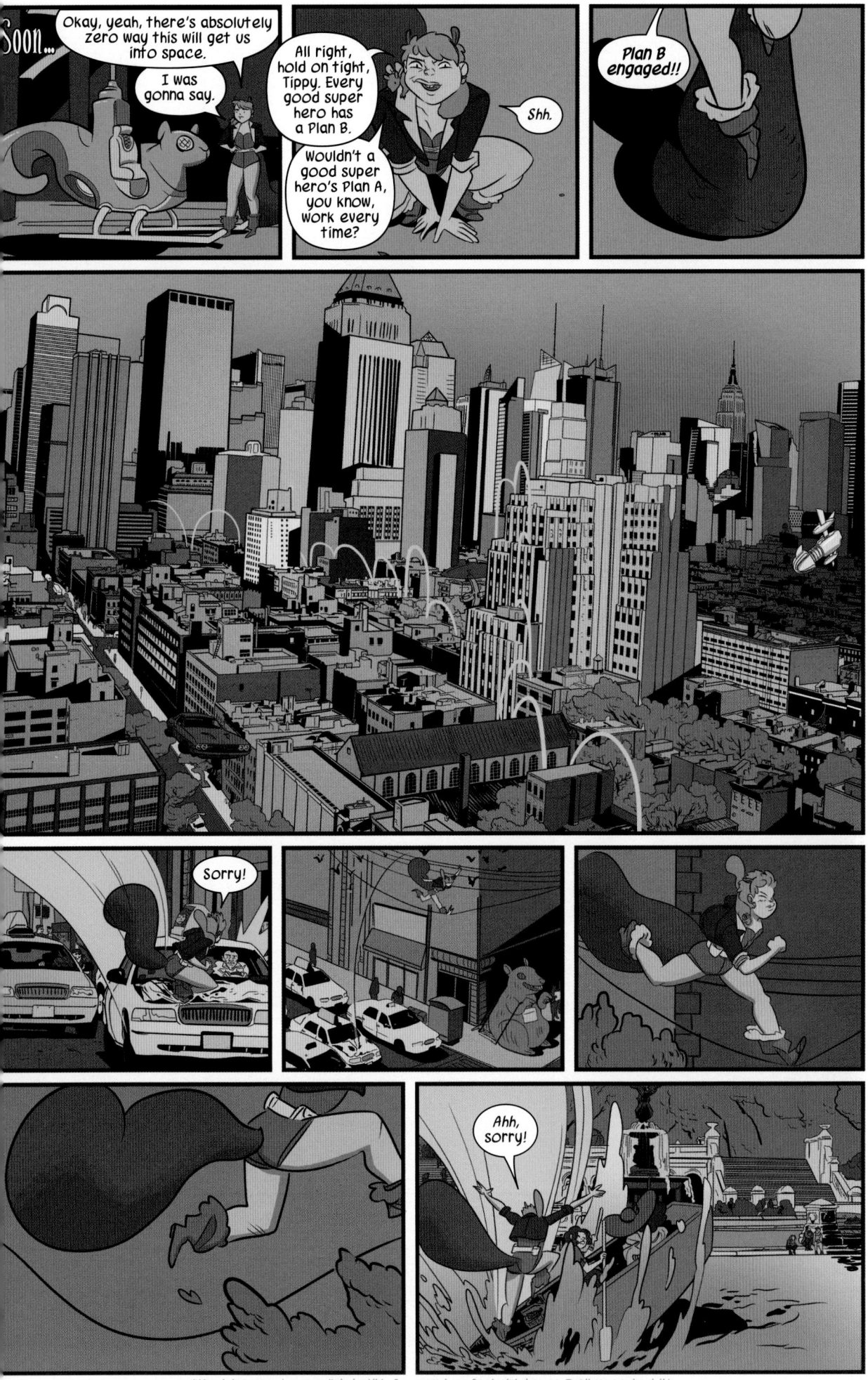

NYC cab insurance has a small deductible for super hero footprint damage. Don't worry about it!

Shoulda paid extra to get rid of that "nigh" in front of "unbreakable glass," Tony!

Okay, now breathe through your mouth! That way we can still taste them, so we're not wasting these delicious nuts.

As my Aunt Benjamina used to say, "With great squirrel agility ability comes great squirrel agility **responsibility**."

All I'm saying is, if these Iron Man robots are anything like my phone, then they cost way too much and don't work very well after you drop them in the toilet.

That "PHWEEEEEeeee" is the sound of the repulsors charging up. The robots aren't saying the "PHWEEEEEeeee" noises themselves, although that would've been *kinda adorable.*

I didn't let you, the reader, know her plan before now because it's a better narrative surprise this way! *Also:* how do I know I can trust you, huh?? You could be *literally anyone.*

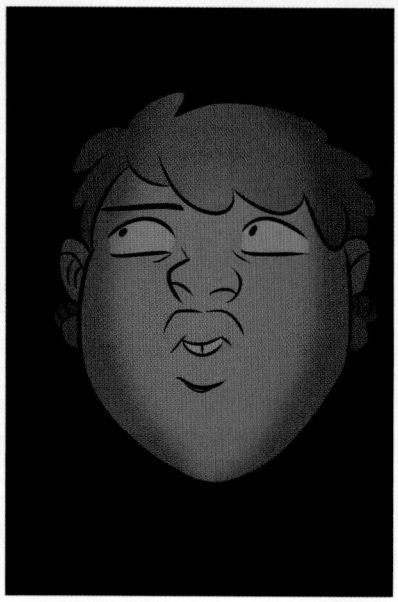

BODY TYPE: Rad / TAIL TYPE: Unexpected / CLAW TYPE: Geez, Tony, you really need to get these nails under control.

e choose to go to the Friggin' moon! We choose to go to the Friggin' moon in these suits and do the other things, not because they is easy, but because they are awesome. Also, if we don't, the planet will get eaten. So, lots of reasons, really.

Next month: *Galactus* and *Whiplash* vs *a woman in a robot suit she borrowed.*

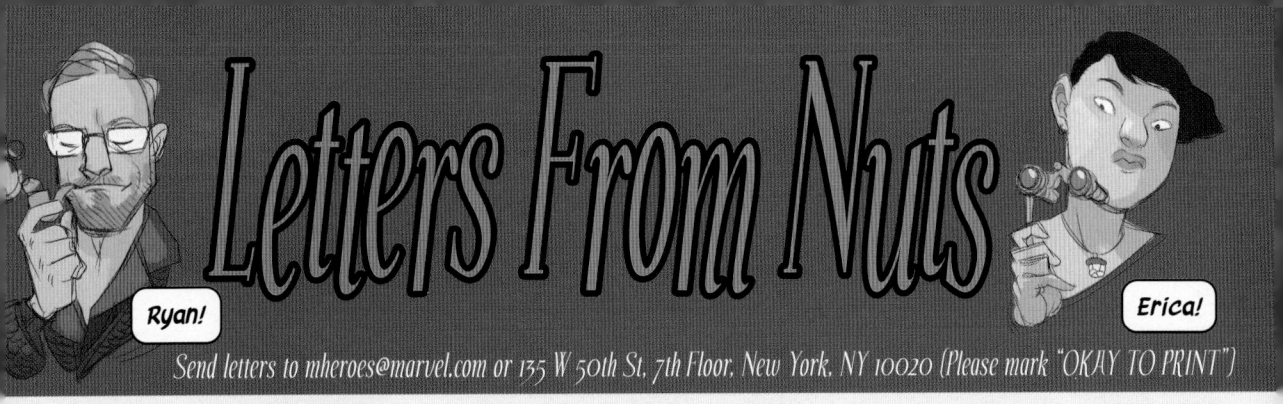

Last month we said all the letters were fake ecause you hadn't sent us any yet, but now we ave TONS and all the letters are real! We love hear from you: send your email to MHEROES@ IARVEL.COM, and don't forget to mark "OKAY TO RINT" in there somewhere. And be sure to follow ur production blog at unbeatablesquirrelgirl. umblr.com! We post fan art, sneak peeks, ketches, recordings of Squirrel Girl's theme song e made in our kitchens - all sorts of fun stuff!

YOUR LETTERS:

Q: In issue #1's letters you wrote, "Can a book ke this find an audience?" We live in a post-Superior oes of Spider-Man world; more and more we eaders like having the "comic" in our comics. You've ound an audience in this guy, that's for sure! Was Ryan/Erica or the editors who wrote the subscript otnotes? Because that was NUT a bad idea. I hope e footnotes are a continued part of the comic mag!

- Trent H.

A: Yeah, that was me (Ryan) doing that! I like e idea of secrets that you get to discover when you ead a comic, and I really hope there are people ho only noticed those secret words halfway hrough (or perhaps, just now, as they're reading his, and now they're going back to see what they nissed?). They will continue forever because I ove writing them forever!

Q: Squirrels. Cannot. Give. You. RABIES!!! Look t up!! Doreen would have known this and corrected er new roommate (even if she didn't know about the squirrel observatories).

-Benjamin G.
True Squirrel Fan

A: ATTENTION EVERYONE: I looked into this nd BENJAMIN IS CORRECT. Squirrels don't even ormally GET rabies, because to get it they'd have o hang around with animals that typically carry it, nd most of those animals try to eat all the squirrels hey see. Squirrel bites are apparently one of the ew animal bites that don't trigger a hospital accination protocol! GOOD TO KNOW.

PS: if you get bitten by a squirrel, maaaaybe still heck with a doctor just in case? You know, before ou take the medical advice you found in the letters age of a comic book.

ERICA: I have personal experience with this, ctually. As a young teenager, I think you call them weens now, during the time when most Marvel characters gain their superhuman abilities, I was itten by a squirrel. I was tested, but did not get abies. We did not test for radiation. It might have een a radioactive squirrel. If you ask, I'll show you ny scar.

Q: Thank you, Erica, for drawing Squirrel Girl not like a sex symbol (I feel awkward when I discovered about she and Logan...). And thank you, Ryan, for showing us that Squirrel Girl is a geek too. It's good to read comics about a girl who is a fan of comics too, and a little tomboy (I'm a tomboy girl too).

Will we see romance between Speedball and Squirrel Girl? I know we are gonna see a lot of Marvel stars in this comic. But I hope to see those love birds together again.

- ScarlettShana

A: Aw, thanks! I wouldn't worry about that Wolverine thing though: all we knew for SURE is that she and Wolverine at one point agreed to never see each other again. BUT NOW I CAN TELL YOU WHY: several years ago, Doreen was about to get into a cab when Wolverine ran up and hopped inside, stealing it from her. Squirrel Girl was (understandably) SUPER-CHEESED and shouted that he was a jerk and his jerkiness must have its OWN healing factor and that she never wanted to see him again. As the cab drove off Wolverine rolled down the window and shouted "You too, bub!". And that's why things were awkward when they met again! THE END.

As for romance with Speedball, everyone has a little romance in their lives at some point, right? But I have a feeling Doreen might have feelings for someone new now...

ERICA: You're welcome, but honestly I just drew her the way I saw her and I don't see her as a sexy character. She's not exactly Emma Frost, you know?

Q: Does Doreen have a flying squirrel costume that opens up and lets her glide?

- Simon S.

A: SPOILER ALERT (IF YOU'RE READING THIS COMIC FROM BACK TO FRONT, THAT IS): She gets an Iron Squirrel outfit this issue, so - kinda! But a base-jumping suit would be PRETTY AMAZING for her to get down the road.

ERICA: Well, I know that S.H.I.E.L.D. has had base-jumping suits for decades and Dum Dum Dugan did invite Doreen to join S.H.I.E.L.D. at one point, so she might have access to some later...

Q: First off, I have to say how absolutely MARVELous (ha!) the first issue of Unbeatable Squirrel Girl was! Wow! Artwork and writing combined, it's pretty much the most perfect comic book of all time and space. Secondly, I have to say how super AWESOME it is to have another female-fronted book, but also one where the character is hilarious and clumsy and endearing and basically a lot more like me than any of the other beautiful, graceful super-women out there. (I love them too, though!) I love everything you've done and I absolutely canNUT wait for the next issue! (One day I'll stop with the puns. Today is NUT that day.)

- Holly R.

A: Thank you! One thing both Erica and I discovered while making this book is how often every day (without thinking!) we would say something is "nuts" or "nutty" or how we'd like "acorn" ("a corn") for dinner. The puns come almost TOO easily!

ERICA: My main thing is I like to draw heartier super ladies, if their powers are mostly physical, because I feel like I shouldn't be able to take down a super hero by sitting on her.

Q: Is it true Squirrel Girl would've been in Avengers 2, but Ultron was too chicken to fight her?

- Andy D.

A: That movie isn't even out yet! How do you know she's NOT in it?? ...But on the off chance that for some reason she isn't, yeah, probably that's the reason! I'm guessing the after-credits scene is just Ultron peeking around corners to make sure Squirrel Girl isn't there, then wiping his forehead and saying "PHEW! CLOSE CALL."

ERICA: I don't know about that, but they need to add her to the movies soon because who's going to take down Thanos???

That's all we have room for, but look for a double-sized letters page next issue! See y'all next month! Stay nutty!

When you see this: AR, open up the MARVEL AR APP (available on applicable Apple ® iOS or Android ™ devices) and use your camera-enabled device to unlock extra-special exclusive features!

3

Doreen Green isn't just a first-year computer science student: she secretly also has all the powers of both squirrel and girl! She uses her amazing abilities to fight crime **and** be as awesome as possible. You know her as...**The Unbeatable Squirrel Girl!** Let's catch up with what she's been up to until now, with...

Squirrel Girl *in a nutshell*

Squirrel Girl! @unbeatablesg
Did you guys see how I took care of Kraven the other day?

xKravenTheHunterx @unshavenkraven
NOBODY LISTEN TO @unbeatablesg, SHE DIDN'T TAKE CARE OF ME, I MERELY DECIDED TO STOP FIGHTING HER

Squirrel Girl! @unbeatablesg
@unshavenkraven hey dude did you kill any gigantos underwater like I suggested?

xKravenTheHunterx @unshavenkraven
@unbeatablesg listen

xKravenTheHunterx @unshavenkraven
@unbeatablesg these things take time

Squirrel Girl! @unbeatablesg
Apparently I'm the only one that can see that GALACTUS IS COMING TO EARTH!!

Tippy-Toe @yoitstippytoe
CHIT CHUKKA CHITTY

Squirrel Girl! @unbeatablesg
Apparently me and @yoitstippytoe are the only ones that can see GALACTUS IS COMING TO EARTH!!

Squirrel Girl! @unbeatablesg
Oh well

Squirrel Girl! @unbeatablesg
guess we'll just have to stop him ourselves then

Squirrel Girl! @unbeatablesg
ON THE FRIGGIN' MOON

Tony Stark @starkmantony
Whoever "borrowed" Iron Man armor parts from my NYC offices, please return them. Looking at you, @unbeatablesg.

Squirrel Girl! @unbeatablesg
@starkmantony Tony it's REALLY IMPORTANT. Like COSMIC important.

Squirrel Girl! @unbeatablesg
@starkmantony I don't know why I'm being coy. It's for Galactus.

Squirrel Girl! @unbeatablesg
@starkmantony I'm gonna beat up @xGALACTUSx, Tony!! ON THE MOON

Tony Stark @starkmantony
@unbeatablesg You break it, you bought it.

Whiplash @realwhiplash22
I JUST WHIPPED @STARKMANTONY OUT OF THE SKY WITH MY ENERGY WHIPS YES YES #OWNED

Tony Stark @starkmantony
Wasn't me. I'm in San Francisco, @realwhiplash22.

Whiplash @realwhiplash22
@starkmantony SORRY I CANNOT HEAR YOU OVER HOW BADLY YOU GOT #OWNED

search!

- #OWNED
- #everythingisnormalinspace
- Welcome to
- #USG
- Number Three
- Hope you like falafel jokes

If you want to stop reading this comic to go get some Falafel, I understand. In fact, I might join you!

Dang, you guys, these Falafel I got are Friggin' delicious!! This is why comics are the best: you can pause at any time to go eat Falafel, so check and mate, ***all other media***. Except books, I guess. ***Fine,*** books are good, too.

Okay, real talk: if you look it up online, you'll find Galactus's *actual* name is "Galan." I'm not joking, it's Galan. Galan A. Lactus.

Wait, this makes two Russian nationals that Doreen has faced off against in as many issues! Looks like these comic issues have their *own* not-so-comic issues, am I right??

Excuse me, but I'm "Whiplash." "Whip-Man" is just an annoying friend of mine with some cheap knock-off of my very expensive technowhips.

This isn't actual American Sign Language, but if you can think of a better hand symbol for "Galactus" then I'm, *um,* all ears.

You know what happens to a squirrel when it gets mad? *The same thing that happens to everything else.*
Which is to say, increased heart rate, elevated adrenaline and norepinephrine production, a lessened capacity for self-monitoring, etc., etc.

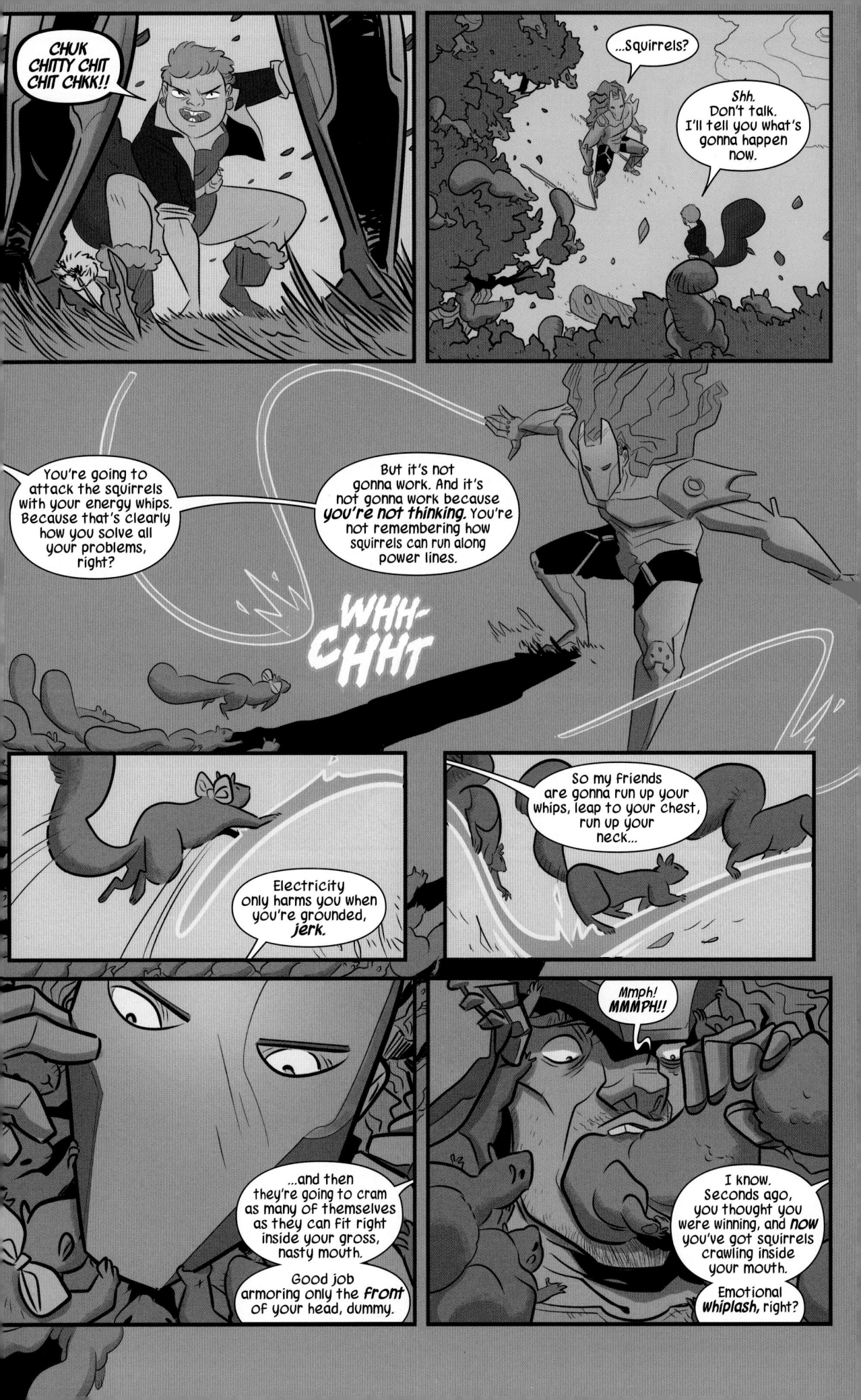
CHUK CHITTY CHIT CHIT CHKK!!
...Squirrels?
Shh. Don't talk. I'll tell you what's gonna happen now.
You're going to attack the squirrels with your energy whips. Because that's clearly how you solve all your problems, right?
But it's not gonna work. And it's not gonna work because you're not thinking. You're not remembering how squirrels can run along power lines.
WHH-CHHT
Electricity only harms you when you're grounded, jerk.
So my friends are gonna run up your whips, leap to your chest, run up your neck...
...and then they're going to cram as many of themselves as they can fit right inside your gross, nasty mouth.
Good job armoring only the front of your head, dummy.
Mmph! MMMPH!!
I know. Seconds ago, you thought you were winning, and now you've got squirrels crawling inside your mouth.
Emotional whiplash, right?

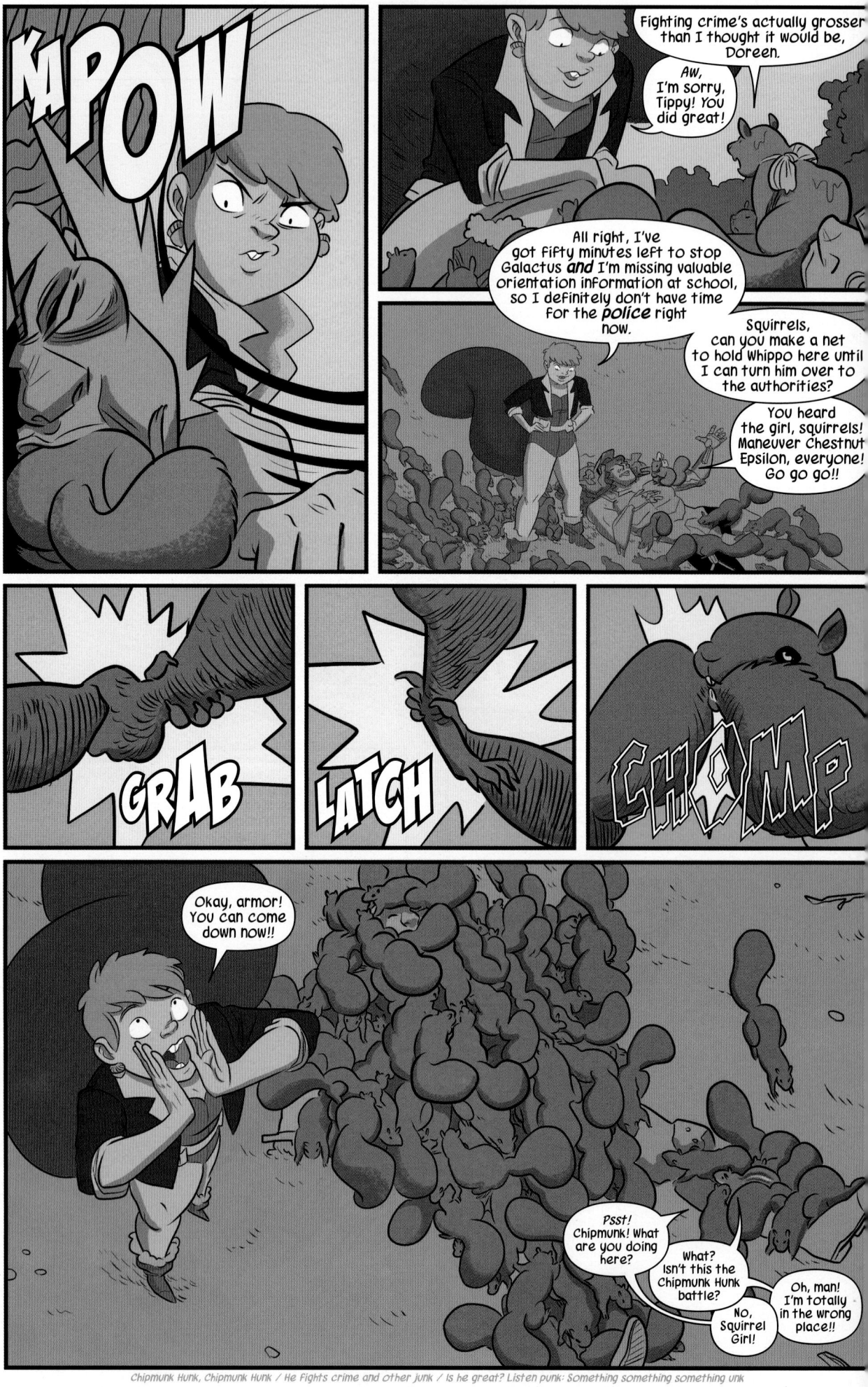

Chipmunk Hunk, Chipmunk Hunk / He fights crime and other junk / Is he great? Listen punk: Something something something unk

To hiiiiim, he is a great big chipmunk / Wherever there's some street punks / You'll find the Chipmunk Hunk!

All right, sorry, I just got excited about Chipmunk Hunk.
Back to Squirrel Girl, huh? But she's not even on this page. *Sheesh!*

Attention, all units: be on the lookout for sucky Larrys in the area. Subjects are to be considered potentially armed and definitely sucky.

In retrospect, Wikipedia *did* mention that groups of squirrels could combine to form giant squirrel-based objects, but I just assumed it was vandalism. I was a fool. A fool!!

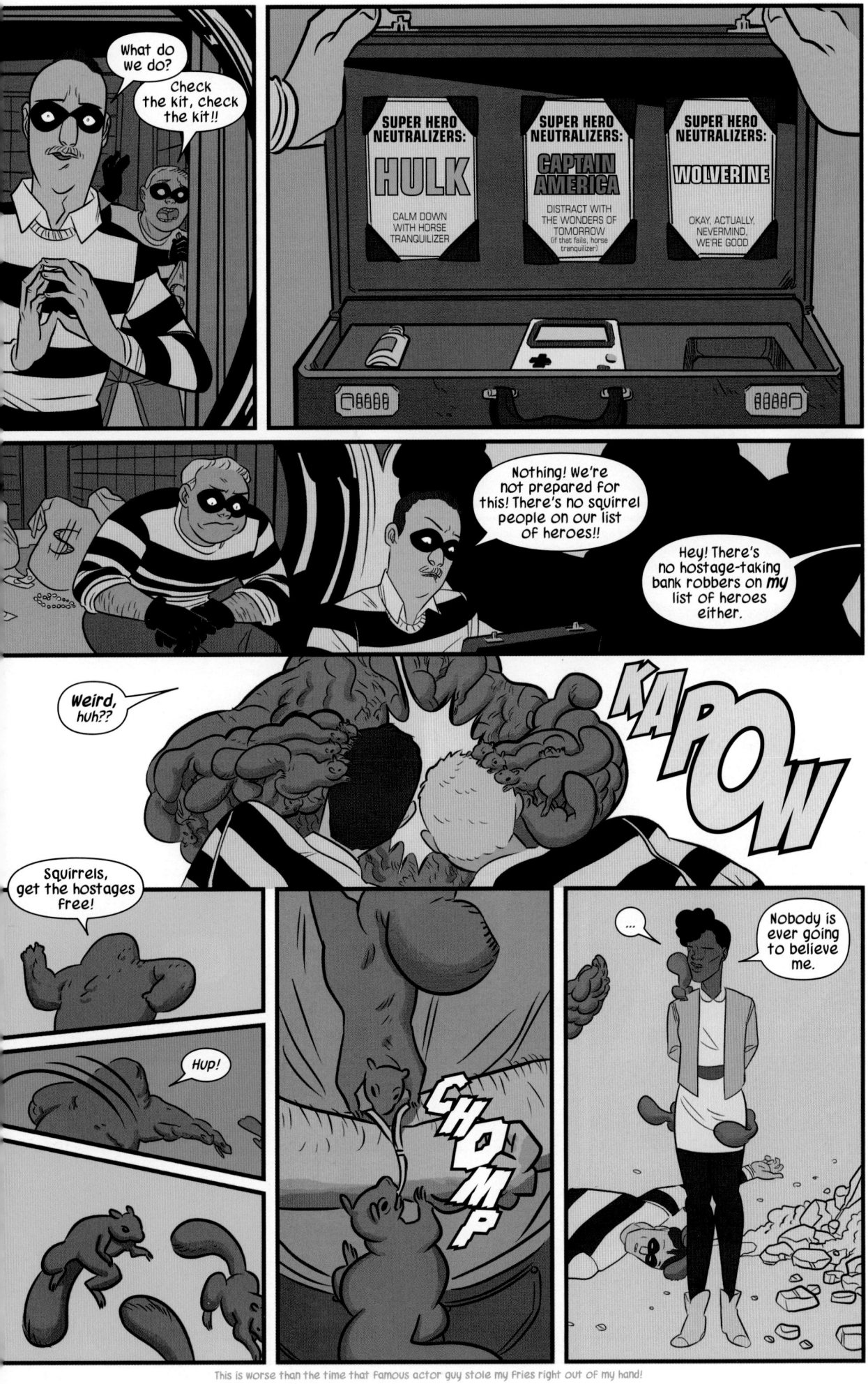

This is worse than the time that famous actor guy stole my fries right out of my hand!

How many other squirrels wear pink bows? Is it a lot? I never really noticed squirrels until now.

It's almost like we're fighting a literal force of nature given squirrel form! But hah hah hah THAT'S CRAZY

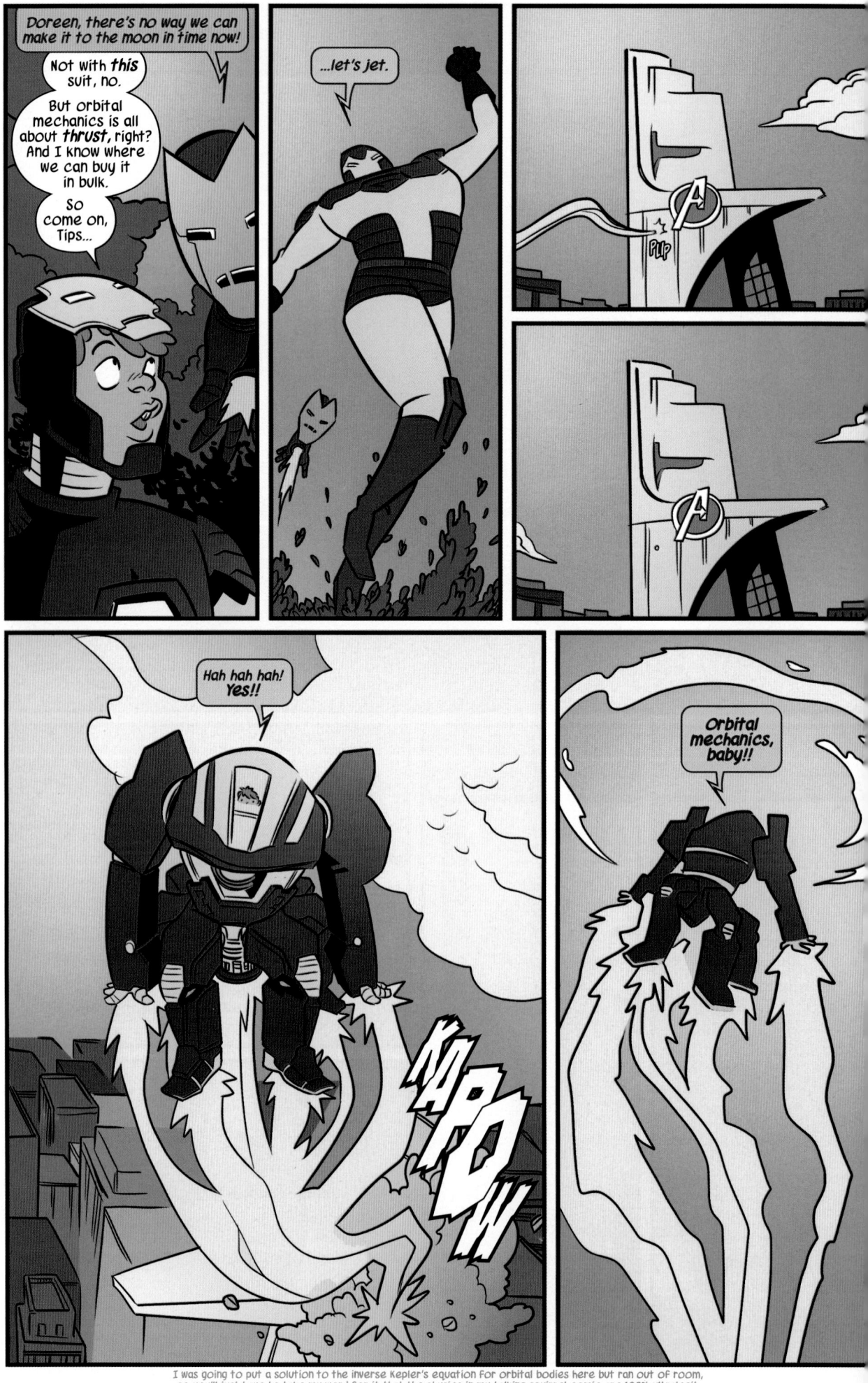

I was going to put a solution to the inverse Kepler's equation for orbital bodies here but ran out of room, so you'll just have to take my word for it that the physics in my talking squirrel comic are 100% ultralegit

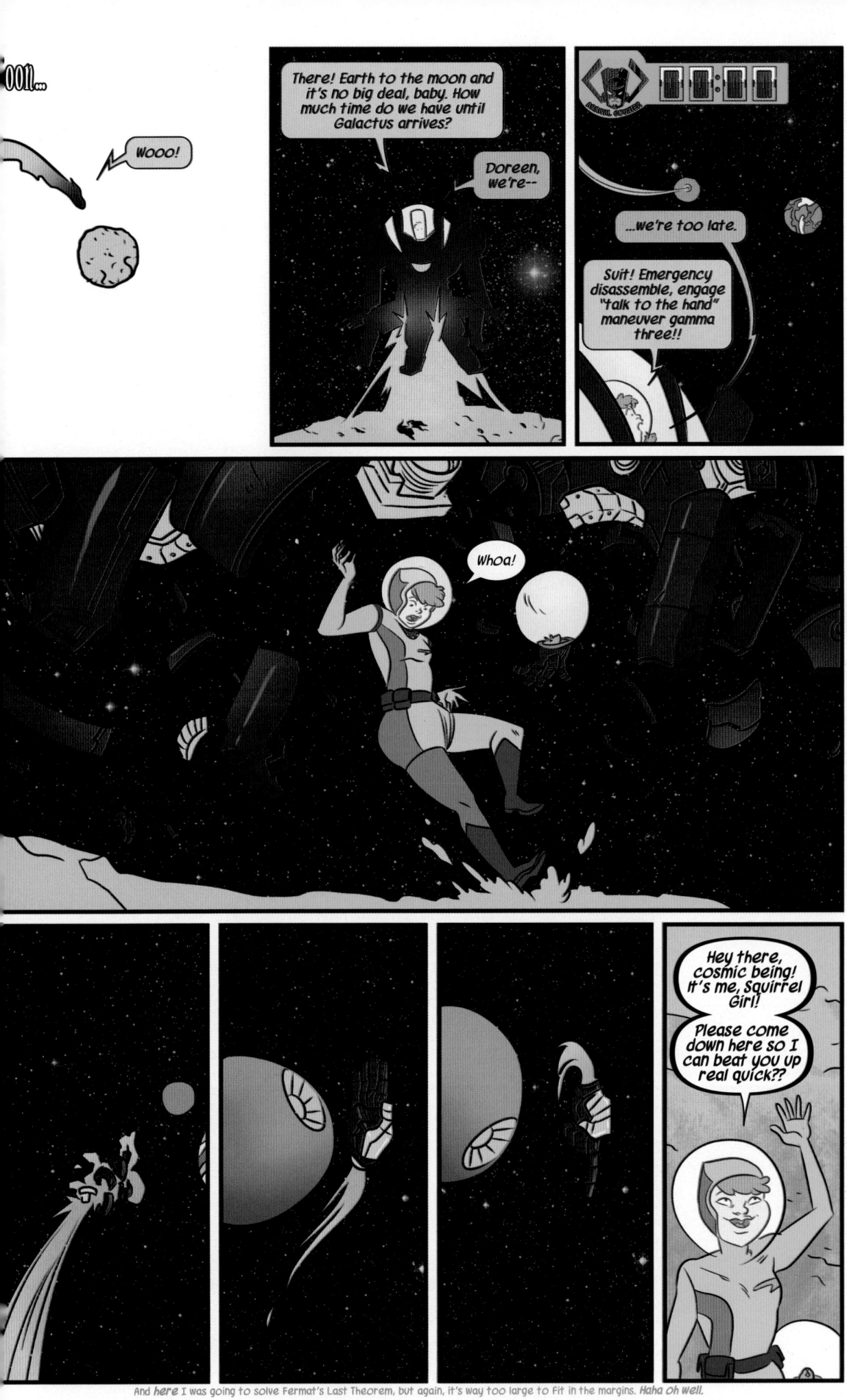

And *here* I was going to solve Fermat's Last Theorem, but again, it's way too large to fit in the margins. *Haha oh well.*

What are you reading down here for? They're about to fight!!

Welcome to the special triple-sized you-guys-are-awesome-and-are-really-vocal-about-your-feelings-for-this-book letters page!!!

Q: Do squirrels and kitties usually get along? Are you concerned that Tippy-Toe and Mew will come to blows?

Michelle K.

RYAN: They don't usually, I think! But Tippy-Toe and Mew aren't your usual squirrel and kitten. Besides, Nancy would never have said it was okay for Tippy-Toe to stay with them unless she was already PRETTY SURE Mew was on board.

Dear Ryan, Erica, Rico, & VC's Clayton (or just Clayton, idk),

You guys, your Squirrel Girl comic is the coolest! Ryan, I've followed your writing online for a number of years, and have been SUPER PUMPED to see you busting out of the internet and on to printed paper held together by staples!

Can we expect to see some Asgardian tomfoolery within these pages? I demand a Doreen vs. Thor/Tippy-Toe vs. **[CENSORED]** throwdown/team-up! I mean, come on, Norse mythology has **[MEGA CENSORED]** (whose name, I learned today, means **[YES, THIS TOO IS CENSORED]** which is pretty cool)! How are you NOT going to use that?!

Keep up the amazing work, everybody!

Adam Barnett
Portland, OR

RYAN: Thanks, Adam! We are actually planning to see that person you mentioned showing up down the line, so I just went ahead and censored your letter here as to not spoil the surprise. I'm sorry! But when it happens you can say "See? CALLED IT" and point to this page for proof. Attention future generations: ADAM WAS TOTALLY RIGHT.

ERICA: Hah! That character might have been the topic of my first frantic middle-of-the-night email to Ryan about Squirrel Girl matters. My first foray into self-publishing was a little bestiary and [REDACTED] is totally in there. I love that dude.

Dear Nutty Buddies,

Thanks so much for producing a title that I can confidently share with my niece, Paislee!

We're both nuts for Squirrel Girl and it's refreshing to know there's a strong, positive, female role-model out there in the Marvel Universe for her to admire on a monthly basis as she grows from being just a tiny little acorn herself.

Here's a question for you: Did you know that in Norse mythology there was **[CENSORED FOR THE EXACT SAME REASONS AS THE LAST LETTER]**? Really! **[THIS OTHER BIT IS CENSORED TOO. EVERYONE, YOU ARE TOO GOOD AT GUESSING OUR STORY IDEAS]** - and then **[AGAIN, CENSORED, SORRY, I GUESS??]**.

Nuts over you,
Paislee H. & Darryl E.

RYAN: Paislee is adorable! #1 Paislee fan over here. Also: I'm glad we're putting out a book you can share with her once she's old enough to realize that if she looks at a certain idiosyncratic series of squiggles in the right order she can hear a voice in her head telling her a story! Once that happens we will be ALL OVER that.

Hi Team Squirrel Girl!

My friend and I just finished the first issue and we both loved it! But we are concerned about Squirrel Girl! Will she have time to go to her classes with all of the crime-fighting that she'll be doing? What are her classes? Thanks!

Beck and Bida

RYAN: I haven't seen her full course selection, but I know there's Introduction to Database Systems, Introduction to Compilers, Linear Algebra, Punching Dudes 101, etc. But yeah, it's tough to balance your social life and your studies. That's why I recommend crime-fighting students cultivate arch-enemies whose powers can dovetail nicely into your education. For example, a super villain who along with trying to take over the world also constructs linear equations in n-dimensional Euclidean vector spaces would be ideal, because that way you can LEARN as you TURN him away from his life of crime.

Q: Now that Squirrel Girl is in college, will she join any clubs or sports teams?

Zachariah W.

RYAN: Zachariah, you clearly wrote this letter before issue #2, where we saw her attempts to join some clubs! So since your question has already been answered, I'm gonna pretend you asked a different question. LIKE SO:

Q: Squirrel Girl has the proportional speed and strength of a squirrel, so what would happen if she got shrunk? Would she lose her powers?

Zachariah W.

RYAN: Excellent question, Zachariah!! This question has not been asked before and I'm glad you definitely came up with it on your own just now. The answer is that while her speed and strength are proportional TO her normal size, they don't change WITH her size. If Ant-Man shrunk her, she'd still be super tough. Similarly, if she ate a bunch and got heavier, that wouldn't make her any stronger. It's too bad, because that would be the EASIEST and MOST FUN way to enhance your super powers ever!

Q: What breed of squirrel is Tippy-Toe? There are 256 species of squirrel worldwide so it's pretty hard to narrow it down.

Sarah Yu
Hong Kong

Squirrel Enthusias

RYAN: Sarah, I'm glad that as a Squirre Enthusiast there is finally a comic for you! don't know what species of squirrel Tippy-Toe is because while I too am a Squirrel Enthusiast, I ar a rank amateur. Are there any Professional Squirre Enthusiasts who can determine Tippy-Toe's exac squirrel type out there?? (No, "rad type" does nc count as an answer.)

ERICA: WELL. I think as someone who gel paid to think about and draw squirrels, I can cour myself as a Professional Squirrel Enthusiast, Ryar Tippy-Toe joined the team after the untimely deat of Monkey Joe (RIP) while Doreen was a membe of the Great Lakes Avengers, who are based ou of Milwaukee. Wisconsin has five varieties c tree squirrel: grey, fox, red, northern flying an southern flying. Tippy is clearly a grey squirre Fun fact: Grey is a variety and does not necessaril reflect the actual color of individual animals.

Dear Ryan, Erica, and Rico,

THE UNBEATABLE SQUIRREL GIRL #1 has to b one of the best comic books I've ever read. It wa funny, cool, quirky, wacky, and a lot of other goo things. Thank you for giving us such an awesom comic book with great art and writing. It's nice t have another super-heroine who doesn't go aroun fighting crime in her underwear. Some people thir the art is "too cartoonish" but 'TIS NOT TRUE! TH ART IS PERFECT!

The Mighty M

P.S. Where can I read Nancy's Cat Thor fa fiction? And where can I get that Purl Jam poster?!

RYAN: Thanks! I actually really like ho Squirrel Girl dresses in layers, because you got figure sometimes it'd get too hot or too cold an you'd want to be able to adjust. It's just sensible As for Nancy's fan fiction epic Cat Thor: Cat God c Cat Thunder, I'd love to have that show up at som point, but for now it lives only in our dreams of better, impossibly perfect world.

ERICA: Ahhhhhh! Thank you so much! I thin clothing choices are pretty important in gettin across who someone is. Some people do want t run around in their underwear and that's great fc them (looking at you, Emma and Namor), but that not everyone's bag. I don't want to get too dee into it but our clothing choices say a lot about wha we want to get across to people, even if you're nc actively thinking about what you're putting on at th time. I mean, you still had to go out and buy it, o if you're a super hero, probably MAKE IT. I war the clothes to feel like something those character would choose for themselves.

Hey guys!

Keep up the good work with Squirrel Girl. It refreshing to see a female super hero that has th body type a lot of us girls have. How did you guy come up with the character design?

Can't wait to read more!

Alex

ERICA: For the body, I didn't think about it much I tend to draw super heroines with more physica powers thicker because I honestly have a har time believing that a 90-pound woman can tak down a 200-pound steroidal dude who has equa fighting ability. So yeah. Her body type in the boo is the same as the first finished drawing of her

ver did because that's just how I see Squirrel Girl. esides, have you seen people who do crossfit? neir thighs are HUUUUUGE.

ey gang,

I rarely if ever write in to comics but I had to drop line regarding SQUIRREL GIRL #1 to let you guys now I think it's great stuff. I've been a fan of SG nce the GREAT LAKES AVENGERS specials back in e day and it's nice to see the character step out into er own series. My hope was that this would be a turn to fun comics without the gloom and grit teeth prevalent in most titles on the stands and I am appy to report you guys hit it out of the park with a nny, entertaining read. Kudos!

Galactus in the second issue? Nice. I guess anklin Richards is going to need a new herald after G gets through with him, huh? I think a college orm lacks the space for a trophy room to keep the ant purple moon boots, so a headquarters might oon be an item on Doreen's To-Do List. . .

Thanks again for a great comic!

Take care,
Stacy Dooks

This book is so much fun. I had no earthly intention f buying it, I liked the character, and I really enjoyed e Dan Slott GREAT LAKES AVENGERS miniseries om a decade ago, but Squirrel Girl as a lead? My udget is paper thin, and I didn't even consider it. But en the reviews came pouring in, all overwhelmingly ositive. And I thought about how disillusioned I've ecome as a comics fan. Neverending event series, e-in series to the events, ret-cons, deaths that last x months to spike sales, major changes to flagship haracters that everyone knows won't last, another n She-Hulk series getting cancelled, FANTASTIC OUR getting shelved, I'm sick to death of it. I thought his might be what I need." Something purely fun, napologetically upbeat.

So I bought it, and I laughed out loud at nearly very page. It was so funny. This is exactly what I eeded right now. A comic to remind me why I ove comics. And now Squirrel Girl is going to fight alactus. This is going to be incredible. You could do n issue where she does nothing but converse with ippy-Toe while onlookers look on in bewilderment, nd I would love it. Between this and ANT-MAN 1, this has been the most enjoyable week I've had eading comics in at least a decade, I'm completely erious. I truly hope the fanboys and fangirls sample his book, because if they do, it will last.

Jason Smith
Buena Park, Ca

RYAN: Jason this is the nicest! You sure know ow to make a guy feel good about his squirrel lady omic: thank you. Our secret is we're just making he sort of book we'd like to read, and we've been eally lucky that other people want to read it too. Hooray for comics!

ERICA: I think it's been said before, but I think e were all worried/curious about the reception of his book. It's definitely different from what people ssociate with mainstream comics so I'm glad that ou like it and that we can fill that gap for you.

Dear Ryan North, Eric Henderson, and the Squirrel irl gang,

I always loved Squirrel Girl and was sad to see ow it wasn't appearing as a solo issue in recent ears. As a result, when I heard that Squirrel Girl was etting its own series I was jumping up and down like squirrel would seeing an acorn!!! The art also brings ut the best of the college story of Squirrel Girl. It is wesome seeing how Squirrel Girl isn't depicted as dark, gritty super hero, but a cheerful, just super ero and the art brings out the best of that. I really am onored to be reading this issue and I wish this story ontinues on forever!!! The jokes make me laugh a t and her cheerful attitude makes me blissful too!

Thanks,
Andre Lee

P.S. I totally love squirrels in real life too!

RYAN: Thanks Andre! Funny thing about squirrels in real life: I never noticed them before, and now I see them EVERYWHERE. So I'll be walking my dog Chompsky to the park and see squirrels in the trees and think "Oh right I'm late on the issue #5 script, I should get on that." So now there's these reminders for me to get back to work distributed WORLDWIDE, on every continent except Antarctica.

Therefore I'm moving to Antarctica, see y'all later!!

Dear Ryan & Erica,

When in 1933 a bunch of newspaper comic strips were put together in a periodical, thus creating the first comic book, if its creators could only know that it would one day lead to THE UNBEATABLE SQUIRREL GIRL, they would have reveled with paroxysms of joy, knowing with happy certainty that they had played such a crucial role to the betterment of Western Civilization.

I could go on, but I fear I might start to tilt toward a touch of hyperbole.

Gene Popa

RYAN: One of my favorite things to think about is how your entire life has technically been leading up to THIS one moment, right now. So if I've just made a good sandwich, my entire life has been leading up to that one delicious sandwich. Then a few seconds later my life has been leading up to me eating it, then cleaning up the dishes, etc. Anyway, Gene: my ENTIRE LIFE has been leading up to me answering your letter just now. Thank you for sending it in!

To the nut that answers these letters,

I have been waiting years (make that 2) for Squirrel Girl to have her own comic book series and when I finally got my hands on issue #1, I went absolutely nuts! And if THE AMAZING SPIDER-MAN can have a 700 issue run, then surely, THE UNBEATABLE SQUIRREL GIRL can have at least 800...I mean, 001 on the cover does mean there's room for up to 999 issues, right? Which brings me to a totally unrelatable question...I know Squirrel Girl speaks English as well as Squirrel and is going to school to learn to speak 1s and 0s, but does she speak any other languages such as Japanese, Chinese, Spanish, or Chipmunk?

Philip Hanan

RYAN: Hah hah, I did not notice until JUST NOW that our book does have two leading zeros on the cover. It's not issue 1, it's issue 001. So that's 999 comics in total that Marvel expects from us, and at one a month, that's...83 ¼ years?! LET THIS BE A LESSON TO US ALL: always read the contracts BEFORE you sign them, lest you find out in a letters page you have SIGNED THE REST OF YOUR LIFE AWAY.

Still. No regrets!!

ERICA: Did you know that chipmunks are also part of the family *Sciuridae?* They are! They probably speak the same language. PROBABLY.

Q: Will Squirrel Girl ever team up with any female characters to kick some major butt?

Maryam F.

RYAN: Yep! AND HOW.
ERICA: ALL THE BUTTS.

Dear Erica and Ryan and Rico,

I just finished the first issue of THE UNBEATABLE SQUIRREL GIRL and I am vexed. I was wondering: How can I be more like Squirrel Girl? I am neither a girl nor a squirrel and have a severe nut allergy. The doctors say I shouldn't even be alive! What should I do?

Your Scholar,
James Kislingbury

RYAN: Okay first off, if you're going to doctors who say "you shouldn't even be alive," you should get a new doctor. Get one who says "you SHOULD be alive and I'm glad you are, holla" instead. And while you might not be able to be Squirrel Girl, you could still be Chipmunk Hunk!

ERICA: Well, the important thing with squirrels isn't so much nuts as much as they're opportunistic omnivores that can't digest cellulose. So try to find foods that have a lot of protein, carbs and fat.

To the inspired minds behind THE UNBEATABLE SQUIRREL GIRL,

I'm gonna be honest here - Squirrel Girl wasn't a hard sell for me. I like comics, I like squirrels. I'm a girl and I like reading about girls. In the title alone Squirrel Girl has almost everything I like in life (still needs: Oreos, posters, high speed car chases, etc).

So I figured I was going to like SQUIRREL GIRL #1 because HOW CAN YOU NOT and then I read it (as I made my own move to college, funnily enough) and was STILL wowed! I AM IN LOVE! It is so much fun, from start to finish! The dialogue is hilarious, the facial expressions are to die for, and the colors are so vibrant and delightful ajskdlfjkasdfj IT IS SO. GOOD.

I can't wait to see more of Doreen's adventures - crime-fighting! Attending classes! Punching and studying, aw yeah! It's all great. Fingers crossed for a long and happy series for Doreen and co.!

Marley

RYAN: Thanks, Marley! You're RIGHT that we haven't had high-speed car chases yet, but it's been tricky because how often do you see squirrels inside a car? INFREQUENTLY AT BEST. I guess... we could change that?

Guys and Gals,

You're all nuts. Irrevocably and gloriously so. ANT-MAN? SQUIRREL GIRL? Astonishing and unbeatable first issues!

More importantly, my sick four-year-old was so engaged as we read (an edited, age-appropriate version of) these comics out loud to her (along with issues of ROCKET RACCOON and MS. MARVEL, whom she loves); it lends such a positive experience to her being in a hospital. In times past (the early 80s), I actually looked forward to plowing through back issues of EARTH'S MIGHTIEST while recuperating from surgery or high fever. Isn't that nuts?

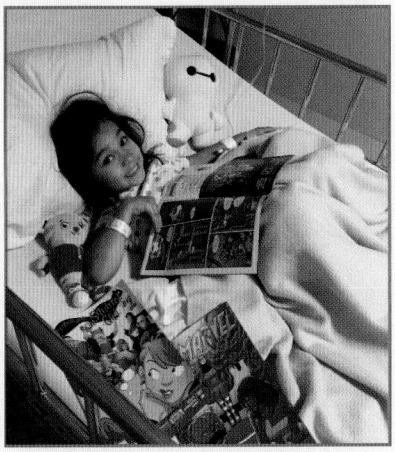

That's probably because every True Believer knows that Marvel Comics are the best medicine.

Nuts, but true.

Papa Joe
Cville, VA

P.S. I do hope Kamala Khan and Doreen Green make it to the MCU!

RYAN: Joe, this is adorable and I wish I got comics when I was sick. I hope your daughter is feeling better and never makes the causal connection between illness and GETTING TO READ ALL THE COMICS EVER, because if I had as a kid I'm sure I'd be faking tummy aches every week.

Dear Erica, Ryan, and Rico,

I've just finished reading issue #1 of your new series and I have to say I absolutely loved it. The humor is spot on, the art is ADORABLE, and she has the best theme song ever.

Also, I've been wondering where I can get myself a pack of those Deadpool super villain trading cards? I could really use them in my top secret crime-fighting endeavors. (Maybe I shouldn't be mentioning this in a, possibly, published letter.)

Sarah Y.
Hong Kong

RYAN: Sarah Y. from Hong Kong, your secret of fighting crime is safe with me! I won't tell anyone that Sarah Y. in Hong Kong fights crime. Also, I would love to see those Deadpool cards in real life

too, but I'm a little worried because then they'd need me to write descriptions for EVERY SINGLE MARVEL VILLAIN EVER IN TIME, which I dunno, might take a while. A long weekend, easy.

First off, thank you so much for giving Squirrel Girl her own comic, it's a breath of fresh air and something I have been waiting for...forever. Because squirrels. Second, yay! The bestest and most awesomest marvel heroine gets some recognition for saving us all from the real threats! Yay again!

Um...this was just a thank you letter really, but if I had to ask questions. Ok. Love the addition of acorn earrings, but have the eye stripes gone for good? They were cute...

Also, any chance we get to meet the parents? Doreen's mum and dad must be the proudest parents, or the most laid back, ever.

I have another thank you, to Ryan and Erica, thank you for giving us an upbeat and completely positive lighthearted book, in an industry where everyone is dark, edgy and gritty. (And depressing... Is it me? Or has every hero got problems? Except Squirrel Girl who has squirrels!)

Love you all!
Tim P.
Plymouth, England.

ERICA: Can you imagine having to take that makeup on and off every time though? Squirrel Girl's back in NYC and there's NO TIME TO STOP FOR ANYTHING.

Dear Squirrel Girl Team,

Hello there, you fabulous people in comic book world! When I heard that they were going to be bringing Squirrel Girl back to the Marvel Universe, I was all filled with glee and dancing a jig. I let that simmer on the back burner, until I heard that Ryan North would be writing it. I can't actually put into print how excited this made me. I guess to go with my previous metaphor, you could say I boiled over. (This is the part where you all are laughing and telling me how clever I am; at least, it is in my head.) I've seen what you can do with six panels of dinosaurs, and I am among those who helped with that Kickstarter of yours for the *Hamlet Choose Your Own Adventure*. Who better to take the helm of this new series?

From the second I pulled the first issue off of the shelf at my comic store, I knew I would not be disappointed. The art is amazing! Doreen didn't look quite how I pictured the new Squirrel Girl to look, but that's okay because she looks even better. I love that pretty much everything is round and colorful. Makes the book so much more approachable to someone like me who is new to the world of comic book buying/collecting. I wish I had a convention coming up so I could cosplay her already. And the story! I want to ask so many questions about where you are heading, but I think I'm just going to wait until the comics come out. Thank you all for your work that you're doing. I look forward to seeing what adventures lay ahead for Doreen and Tippy-Toe. And on that note, I'm off to see if Rosetta Stone offers a course on the Northeastern variant of Squirrelese.

Your Unbeatable Fan,
Stefanie M.

RYAN: Thank you, Stefanie! And I am secretly really excited for convention season this year, because I really want to see the Squirrel Girl cosplay. Everyone dress up as her forever, thanks in advance!!

UNBEATABLE SQUIRREL GIRL was the absolute highlight of my day, week, and possible even year (though it's a little early to tell). I'm so excited to see Doreen not only put bad guys in their place but also tackle the exciting world of Computer Science - how incredibly rad. It's the kind of book that gives me hope for super-hero comics. In the mean time, I have two questions for you:

1) Will any of Doreen's past friends (the GLA, Devil, or the Cage-Jones family) be making appearances?

2) If Doreen could have lunch with any other Marvel super hero who would it be?

Congratulations and I'm sure you'll continue to knock it out of the park.

Arielle B.

RYAN: I know Erica loves Flatman (AND WHO DOESN'T?) so I'd love to have him appear at some point! Of course, who's to say that he hasn't ALREADY appeared, only he was standing at just the right angle as to be invisible? WHO INDEED. Well in fact it's the artists and writers who can say, and we're here saying he hasn't done that in Squirrel Girl.

YET.

ERICA: If Doreen could have lunch with any other hero it would be Dazzler because, oh my god, she has, like, ALL of her albums.

Dear Squirrel Girl Creative Team (can I call you the Squirrel Squad?)

I'm absolutely nuts about Doreen! Thank you for bringing back one of my favorite Marvel characters from obscurity into a book I can shove in all my friends' faces. The first issue was all I hoped it would be and more.

I am foaming at the mouth for the next one already! (I should probably go get that checked out.) I am curious, how did you choose between Tippy-Toe and Monkey Joe to appear in the series?

Amy Chase

Ok I've been obsessed with Squirrel Girl and waiting for this moment for a while now... great job on the first issue! I really wanted her to kick some major butt in the first issue but next one looks pretty crazy so I already can't wait.

I MUST know what her MJ necklace stands for. If it's Marc Jacobs I will die but I think there's another meaning... Also, I need her purse, any idea where I can get one?!

Last, Squirrel Girl needs to go into psychiatry or psychology. She has a way with talking to this guy that shows a gift.

Love,
Squirrel Girl super fan for life

RYAN: It stands for "Monkey Joe," her first squirrel companion! He was the squirrel she hung out with before Tippy-Toe. It could also stand for "My Jewelry," in case she only wears jewelry that describes itself. They only way to confirm that for sure though is if she ever wears earrings that just say "earring," which I think... might be amazing??

ERICA: I totally own a brown version of that purse. I think it's sold out. I'm sorry. I'm just going to be honest here, I pretty much own all of Doreen's clothes.

I want to say "chitter chit chit chitter" THANK YOU for bring Squirrel Girl back. The fact that she wears the MJ in homage to Monkey Joe makes me want to tear up.

I can't wait for the next issue! My squirrel friend Ladro is throwing nuts at me asking how he can join the squirrel army?

Sincerely,
Beth 'the Squirrel' Jankowski

ERICA: I'm glad I'm not the only one who tears up over Monkey Joe. (RIP)

Hi Squirrel Girl Team!

So I'm writing this on a Tuesday night becaus I run a shop and I totally stayed late tonight just t read your book.

I just want to say going in I wasn't convinced. wasn't a fan of the art, but by the second page (tha we hadn't seen in the preview yet) I was totally wo over. I love it! I can't wait to sell this to everyon that comes in tomorrow and days after that until I ru out then I can sell the 2nd and 3rd and 4th printing too, and the hardcovers and trade paperbacks. Thi book rocks and it will be great for anyone that love fun and maybe we can win over some of the peopl that hate fun too.

One little thing, any chance the color on th bottom page tidbits can be altered a teensy bit? The were really hard to read. Or I just need new glasses

Thanks for the fun comic!

Jenn Swackhame
Comic City Pontiac, M

Hello!

First off, I have to say how absolutely MARVELlou (ha!) the first issue of UNBEATABLE SQUIRREL GIR was! Wow! Artwork and writing combined, it's prett much the most perfect comic book of all time an space.

Secondly, I have to say how super AWESOM it is to have another female-fronted book, but als one where the character is hilarious and clumsy an endearing and basically a lot more like me than any c the other beautiful, graceful super-women out there (I love them too though!) I love everything you'v done and I absolutely canNUT wait for the next issue (One day I'll stop with the puns. Today is NUT tha day.)

Holly Ringsel

Well, we've used up all the extra room w have this month! But keep writing! We wan to hear from every dang one of you! And don' forget to check out our behind-the-scenes tumblr unbeatablesquirrelgirl.tumblr.com! See y'all nex month! Stay nutty!

Next: Squirrel Girl vs. Planet-Eating Man!

ISSUE #1 VARIANT COVER BY **SIYA OUM**

the unbeatable Squirrel Girl
VS

Doreen Green isn't just a first-year computer science student: she secretly also has all the powers of both squirrel and girl! She uses her amazing abilities to fight crime **and** be as awesome as possible. You know her as...**The Unbeatable Squirrel Girl!** Let's catch up with what she's been up to until now, with...

Squirrel Girl *in a nutshell*

GALACTUS @xGALACTUSx
HEY GUESS WHAT I'M COMING TO EARTH TO DEVOUR THE ENTIRE PLANET

GALACTUS @xGALACTUSx
AND NOBODY KNOWS BECAUSE I PUT MY SHIP IN A STEALTH FIELD

GALACTUS @xGALACTUSx
"BUT WAIT," YOU SAY, "AHA! NOW WE KNOW YOU'RE COMING BECAUSE YOU JUST POSTED IT ON SOCIAL MEDIA!!"

GALACTUS @xGALACTUSx
ONLY YOU AREN'T SAYING THAT BECAUSE NOBODY KNOWS I'M COMING BECAUSE NOBODY FOLLOWS ME ON THIS STUPID SITE

GALACTUS @xGALACTUSx
...

GALACTUS @xGALACTUSx
#ff @xGALACTUSx

Tony Stark @starkmantony
@unbeatablesg Just heard more of my Iron Man parts have been "borrowed," and now there's a big hole in my building too. Any ideas?

Squirrel Girl! @unbeatablesg
@starkmantony Oh wow dude these suits have wifi in them??? I can go online on my way to the MOON?? Tony ur the best <3

Tony Stark @starkmantony
@unbeatablesg That "wifi" works even in Mars orbit, uses proprietary Stark technology, and costs several thousand dollars a kilobyte.

Squirrel Girl! @unbeatablesg
@starkmantony um I already downloaded some songs for the trip to the moon. Sorry!!!

Tony Stark @starkmantony
@unbeatablesg Don't reply to say you're sorry! That ALSO costs money!

Squirrel Girl! @unbeatablesg
@starkmantony sorry sorry!

Tony Stark @starkmantony
@unbeatablesg Don't reply! Stop replying!

Squirrel Girl! @unbeatablesg
@starkmantony whoooooooooooooooooooooooooooops

Nancy W. @sewwiththeflow
Story time, friends. Your hero, me, thought she'd eat some delicious (cash-only) falafel. So I went to the bank.

Nancy W. @sewwiththeflow
And you know how banks are always the worst even when you're NOT being taken hostage? WELL GUESS WHAT?

Nancy W. @sewwiththeflow
Yep. But then we got saved by @unbeatablesg who appeared in SQUIRREL SUIT ARMOR MODE. Not even joking.

Nancy W. @sewwiththeflow
This really happened. I was saved by a squirrel suit Squirrel Girl. I know you don't believe me.

Nancy W. @sewwiththeflow
tl;dr: doesn't matter, ate falafel

Whiplash @realwhiplash22
I am trapped in #CentralPark and need #squirrelrepellant, PLEASE RT!!!!! #please #rt #please #rt #please #rt

search!

#bankrobbery
#banksnobbery
#mew
#squirrelsuitcrochetpattern
#snackcakes
#squirrelman

All right! Now to the letters page, and then the rest of this book is just blank pages! *Haha,* ***Oh well!!***

Letters From Nuts

Send letters to mheroes@marvel.com or 135 W 50th St, 7th Floor, New York, NY 10020 (Please mark "OKAY TO PRINT")

Dear Squirrel Girl comics,

I really liked Tippy-Toe's squirrel armor. I can't believe that Squirrel Girl's fighting Galactus. I mean, that's a big thing, you know! I find that the cover is very funny because Squirrel Girl is using Iron Man as a surfboard. I mean, a surfboard? That's cray-cray!

Signed,
Elsa McQuaid

RYAN: Thanks! To invent Tippy-Toe's armor I held out my hand in an approximately squirrel shape and confirmed, yes, that would fit inside a glove. And if you're reading this, then you just read the page that showed the aftermath of Squirrel Girl beating Galactus off panel, which we can all agree was really very satisfying! Writing: It's easy!!

ERICA: I remember getting an e-mail saying we needed the second cover and that it should be Squirrel Girl surfing on an Iron Man suit and my first thought was "That's stupid." I'll admit when I'm wrong-- just don't tell Ryan I told you that. Any part of that.

Dear "Letters from Nuts" crew,

As a comic collector of over 20 years, I want to thank you for creating such a great comic. Over the past several years, my love of comics has crossed over with another love: squirrels! I have been a squirrel fanatic since my college days when I worked on an independent study project to identify squirrel parasites. In the last few years, I have been taking a sketchbook to the comic conventions that I attend and I have been asking various artists to draw a Squirrel mashed-up with any character of their choosing! I have attached several of the sketches for your enjoyment (including some of my own):

Question: Based on Marvel's summer plans, is there any way we could get a small landmass on Battleworld assigned to a whole universe where all of the Marvel characters are squirrels (and maybe Squirrel Girl could rule them all)? In my opinion, that would be the most important part of the Secret Wars crossover!

Your loyal fan,
Corey Fuhrer

RYAN: Those pictures are amazing. If only we had made this comic more than one page long, we could've shown you Squirrel Galactus! But alas, we decided to publish this book with only one page of comics, some letters, and then a whole bunch of blank pages.

I have pitched your idea to Marvel and they informed me that it's "way too late" to rewrite their Battleworld plans to include Squirrel Island, although they "wish they had thought of that sooner" and "feel regret about not doing Squirrel Island more keenly than [they] have ever felt any emotion before, including love." So – that's something!

ERICA: Although we SHOULD do Squirrel Island but like Spider Island. (Because let's follow up on ALL of Dan Slott's ideas.) Everyone on Manhattan gets bitten by radioactive squirrels but nobody turns into a Squirrel Girl equivalent because that's not how she got her powers. Pretty sure this is a one-page story. Is NOT BRAND ECHH still a thing?

Is Chipmunk Hunk perhaps a monk? Look, I'm just trying to think of rhymes for the theme song.

Stephen,
Kansas City

RYAN: All I know for sure is: he's been shrunk, he can dunk, spelunk, his car's got a trunk, and if you bring him to a cabin he'll steal the top bunk.

ERICA: RYAN. Leave the rhyming to the professionals. Like Adam WarRock. Have you HEARD his Squirrel Girl rap? (www.adamwarrock.com) Step down, buddy.

My four-year-old twin daughters enjoy squirrels quite a bit. They are always asking if we can leave some peanut butter and crackers outside to feed our neighborhood squirrel crew. They also love comic books, as they've been exposed to them pretty much since they were born. So, it was a no-brainer to hip them to THE UNBEATABLE SQUIRREL GIRL series.

There aren't very many comics that the girls will allow me to read them from start to finish. They generally prefer to tear through 'em on their lonesome, looking at the artwork and making up their own dialogue. SQUIRREL GIRL is one of the exceptions though.

One constant with each issue I've noticed is that they keep asking me where Gamora is. So if you end up having the Guardians of the Galaxy make an appearance, that would seal the deal with their appreciation of Squirrel Girl.

Darrick Patrick
Dayton, Ohio

P.S. I'm including a photograph of Nola and Logann showing off their Unbeatable collection so far:

RYAN: Awesome, a complete set! You can tell Nola and Logann that I, the writer of these comics, say that Gamora is secretly there, just hidden. She and Doreen were going to get lunch together before Doreen got wrapped up in this Galactus thing, so while Doreen's there fighting Whiplash and bank robbers and Galactus, Gamora's standing there, just out of frame, gesturing

to her watch, impatiently waiting.

ERICA: Yes! My favorite compliment this book gets is being able to share it with your kids, so I love that! Side note: peanuts aren't great for squirrels and apparently can get some sort of weird invisible toxic mold (citation needed)??? If you want to leave a snack out, nuts in shells are great. It's something they love and the shell provides good gnawing exercise.

Well Hi there!

This is why I really like Squirrel Girl: she's really funny-looking. On a new-comics wall, I can look across all Marvel's titles; lots of angry-looking, grim but very buff-looking hero-suited figures, and there's Squirrel Girl, happy and goofy-looking. I have to support that. And apparently she's the most powerful super-powered person in the whole Marvel Universe? Y'know, I get a lot of comics, but now I'm down to just two Marvel comics, this one, and Captain Marvel. Guess I just like strong, pleasant women in my life. Carol and Doreen are like that, nice people. One's goofy-looking: y'know? -- in the Marvel Universe, that just makes her exceptional.

It certainly helps that SQUIRREL GIRL's written well. And works well with a slightly 'cartoony' edge to the artwork. The words and pictures really support one-another. You could do me a favor, though, by using a darker ink to your teeny tiny bottom-page typings. Old eyes, y'know? Thanks for a good, fun comic.

Best wishes,
Matt Levin
Hatfield, MA

ERICA: I'm glad you're into it! I really stressed out when I was first asked to draw this character. One of the only pieces of mine that Wil (our editor) mentioned when we were starting out was a much more realistic-looking movie poster I drew, and I went back and forth on how the style should look. In the end I took a gamble on a looser and more animated look and I'm super happy that it's worked out.

Loved, loved, loved UNBEATABLE SQUIRREL GIRL #2. Art and story - killing it! Thank you for this book.

Any chance we'll see the Great Lakes Avengers at some point? I mean, that's where I first met Doreen, and now she's way more popular than the GLA so it'd be nice to use her popularity to bolster them up. Also, when you inevitably get to your big, triple-sized anniversary spectacular, could you reprint her first appearance? It's not an easy "tail" to come by. Thanks!

Charles Albert,
Richmond VA

RYAN: I'd like to! I really like Flatman because he has all the powers of being a man AND all the powers of being flat. I can't tell you how many times I've looked at tiny cracks under doors and wanted to see what was on the other side and said "If only I was a flat, but alas, I am a man." Okay, I can: it's several. I have done that several times.

ERICA: I keep picturing the GLA reunion like a high school reunion and Doreen is the one kid that left their small town to do something big and is home for the first time in 10 years and just has no idea if it's going to be super awkward or not. Also, everyone is worried Deadpool is going to show up. THAT GUY, AMIRIGHT?

I just wanted to thank you guys for starting to write/print this comic at such an opportune time. Just two weeks ago I was mentioning that Squirrel Girl existed to a friend and he didn't really believe me, so I looked her up to show him and simultaneously found out that these were being printed! Now, hopefully, I'll get to show him a physical copy with my name in it! It also gives me a great read to look forward to every week with my best-friend-roommates. So...Thank you for such a humorously written and expertly drawn comic!

On an unrelated note though, any chance of us ever seeing any physical copies of Deadpool's Guide to Super Villains and Super Villain Accessories in the future?

Andre W.

RYAN: I'd love to see the Deadpool cards as a set! I don't know if anyone higher up at Marvel Headquarters reads the letters page of our squirrel comic BUT IF THEY DO: Yo, that's two months in a row people have asked for these cards! Please make them immediately. PS: this counts as market research, and I have never been wrong before.

ERICA: Henderson and North, MAKING IT HAPPEN. (The comic/continuation of Squirrel Girl, not the cards. We don't really have control over merchandising- yet.)

To whom it may concern,

I got the first two issues of UNBEATABLE SQUIRREL GIRL recently, and I can't wait to for next month's issue. Thank you for making Tippy-Toe so cute, and for Nancy. I knit and crochet, too (and now I know next year's Halloween costume). I couldn't resist making a little Tippy-Toe for myself. Thank you for creating something so cute and fun.

Keep up the amazing work!
Katie H.

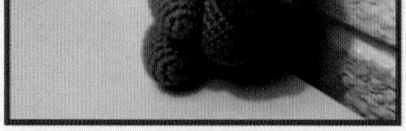

RYAN: Katie, GUESS WHAT: I love that Tippy-Toe so much! Nancy's knitting is inspired by my mom, who made me a sweater with a dinosaur on it, and the sweater has a hood with a tassel, AND THE DINOSAUR ON THE SWEATER IS WEARING THE SAME SWEATER WITH THE SAME HOOD AND TASSEL. It's the best ever.

ERICA: AHHHHH. WHAAAAAT. I do some sewing, but knitting and crocheting are amazing mystery arts to me. I'm so in awe! That Tippy is just so cute! Fun Fact: When I first saw Nancy in the script she was so much like a friend of mine that I grew up with that I had to reread her intro a few times. When issue 1 came out, other friends asked if it was her. So I love tha people are getting into Nancy because she rocks!

Hey guys,

Thanks for making such an epic comic first of all! Secondly, I really like Mew anc also knitting. How can I join Mew Club?

Jane
Cat, Squirrel, and Yarn Enthusias

RYAN: To join Mew Club you have tc write down "Mew is a great cat" on a piece of paper and sign your name, and ther you are a member of Mew Club. Mew is based on two cats we know in real life (one I know, and one Erica knows) and when you perform this ritual, we will be alerted, anc will inform the Actual Mews of this Actua News.

Wanted to say that, as one of two comics I'm reading, this one is my personal favorite Just wanted to ask, have you ever come across negative reception for the comic? How did you deal with it?

Felix

RYAN: Thanks for reading our comic! Also, you should read more comics!

There's always going to be people who don't like what you're doing, and it's like, that's fine? There are books I don't like but I don't hate them or want them destroyed or anything. I just don't read them! So if I see someone reacting negatively to anything I do, I don't take it personally, I just think "Oh that's too bad, this person's tastes are not my own. I guess their opinions are different from my clearly objectively correct ones, oh well."

ERICA: I'm with Ryan. There are going to be some people that you just don't agree with on taste and even if they're jerks about it there's not much you can do there, so there's no point in dealing with that. The only time I address it is when I get "won't read because Squirrel Girl isn't hot anymore" because UGH. Anyway, it's pretty easy to get those dudes to back off with a quick "why are you so concerned about a minor being hot?" Also, I'm so curious about this one other comic you're reading. Tweet us about it when you see this answer!

Next: Readers Beware!

Yep, that hidden message at the bottom of that earlier page was a lie! Downside: *I'm an unreliable secret message narrator.*
Upside: Hey, at least this comic isn't a total ripoff now, right??

SCIENCE CORNER: You're in space right now, too! You're on a ball of *liquid metal* surrounded by rocks and a thin layer of gas, spinning wildly through the universe at thousands of kilometers per hour. Hang on tight!

If the Power Cosmic is anything like an acorn, *and I'm pretty sure it is,* then we should bury it in the ground and then forget where we buried it and then a Power Cosmic tree will grow from that spot many years from now!

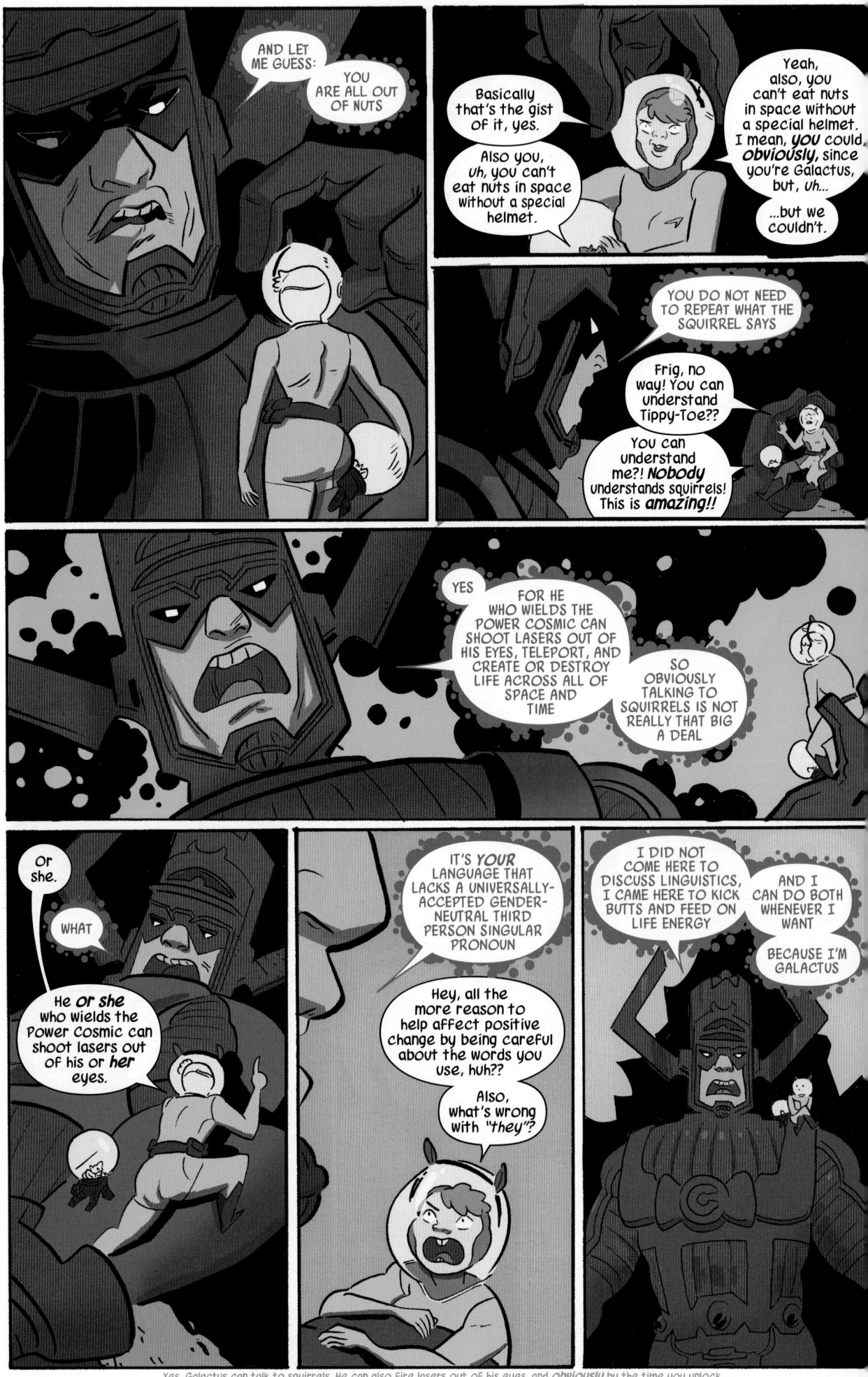

Yes, Galactus can talk to squirrels. He can also fire lasers out of his eyes, and *obviously* by the time you unlock *"Level 1: Laser Eyes"* you've already mastered *"Level 100: Chatting Up Tiny Mammals"!*

EVERYONE WAS ALL "OH LOOK IT'S GALACTUS, I THINK HE'S GREAT BUT THE ONLY WAY I CAN EXPRESS THIS ADMIRATION IS TO STYMIE HIS PLANS, NEVERTHELESS I DO SECRETLY REALLY RESPECT WHAT HE'S TRYING TO DO HERE"

IF YOU SEE HIM, TELL HIM I SAID HE'S SO UNCOOL THAT HE'S NOT JUST A SQUARE...HE'S A COSMIC CUBE

Turns out you ***can't*** defeat Galactus by just chilling with him on the moon! All right, Tippy, scratch that off the list, and we'll see how well *"Fight him in orbit **around** the moon"* works out.

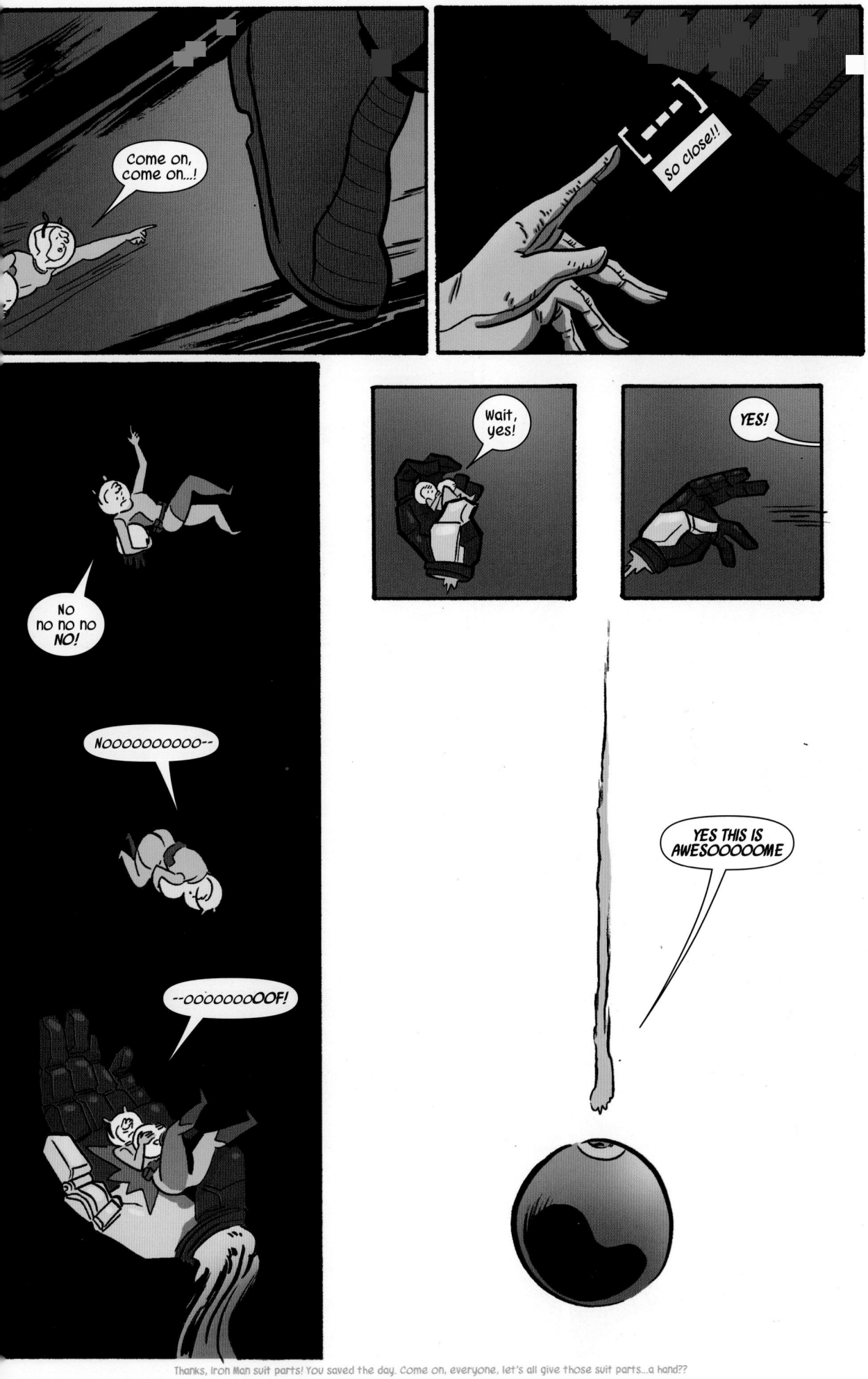

Thanks, Iron Man suit parts! You saved the day. Come on, everyone, let's all give those suit parts...a hand??

Alternate password suggestions: GALACTUSRULES, G@L@CTUSRUL3Z, I<3CONSUMINGALLLIFEENERGY

And you definitely don't defeat Galactus by having a more audacious fashion sense. Many have tried, all have failed, though honestly many of them looked pretty great while they did so.

Galactus, I don't know what your computers actually look like, but that retro computer interface had ultra-primitive terrible security.
Do I thank you, or thank my imagination, or...?

SWOOOF
SWOOOF
On second thought, Galactus, maybe you **should** eat Earth instead of this planet??
Tippy!!
DUDE, I'M SORRY, BUT THIS PLACE IS THE GREATEST!

So in conclusion, then we came back to the moon to lie down because we all over-ate, and here we are!
NO REGRETS

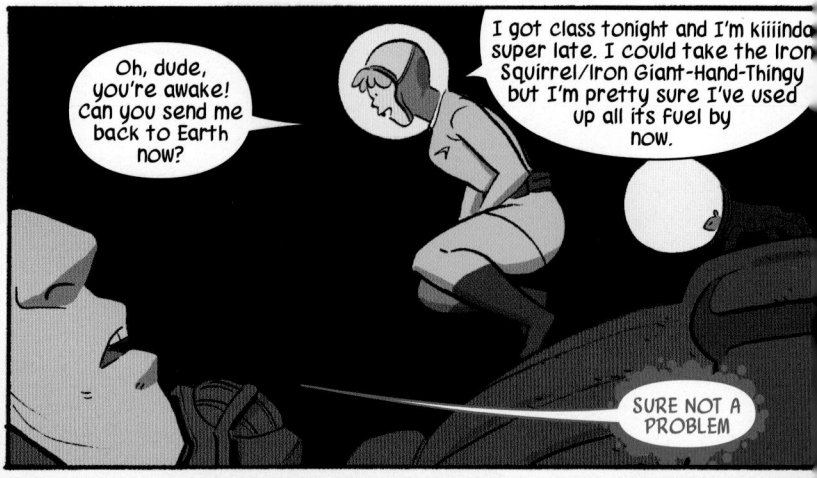
Oh, dude, you're awake! Can you send me back to Earth now?
I got class tonight and I'm kiiiinda super late. I could take the Iron Squirrel/Iron Giant-Hand-Thingy but I'm pretty sure I've used up all its fuel by now.
SURE NOT A PROBLEM

BUT BEFORE YOU GO I WANTED TO GIVE YOU A LITTLE SOMETHING
AND YOU SHOULD KNOW THAT AMONG THE MANY POWERS OF HE--
--OR SHE--
--WHO WIELDS THE POWER COSMIC IS THE ABILITY TO READ MINDS

SO I ALREADY KNOW YOU'LL LIKE IT
No way.
No way.

Oh. Oh, Galactus.

I love it.

DEADPOOL'S GUIDE TO SUPER VILLAINS
CARD 1 OF 1622
GALACTUS
- DEVOURER OF WORLDS
- WIELDER OF THE POWER COSMIC
- ...AND A FRIEND
CALL ME IF YOU EVER WANT TO GET INTO HERALDING.

Well, you're almost out of power, so maybe don't fly. Slowly walk or roll home, Iron Man suits!! You're free now!

Oh, don't worry, that's not you! That's my new 100% original character named "Squirrely D. Girly." TRADEMARK AND COPYRIGHT BY ME, DO NOT STEAL!!

Doreen, do you even know where Ireland is? Doreen, do you need to take Intro to Really Basic Geography before you take Intro to Compilers??

Tomorrow's headline: MYSTERIOUS SQUIRREL MAN SPOTTED WITH CAT?? CAT IS NAMED MEW AND SEEMS KINDA SURLY BUT STILL MEGA CUTE.

Written by
Ryan North

Art by
Erica Henderson

Trading Card Art by
Chris Giarrusso

Color Art by
Rico Renzi

Lettering and Production by
VC's Clayton Cowles

Cover Artist	Erica Henderson
Special Thanks to	Cassie Hart Kelly
Assistant Editor	Jon Moisan
Editor	Wil Moss
Executive Editor	Tom Brevoort
Editor in Chief	Axel Alonso
Chief Creative Officer	Joe Quesada
Publisher	Dan Buckley
Executive Producer	Alan Fine

Squirrel Girl will return in...
Squirrel Girl #5, duh.

I swear, animals, you can let me go now. I promise I won't whip **any** of you.
We understand each other, yes?

Hey, you like nuts, I will get you nuts. So many nuts. I will knock over a bulk food store and give you eighty-five percent of the take, yes?? No, no, **ninety-five** percent.
Animals?

Animals, I really really have to go to the bathroom.

Tails of the unbeatable Squirrel Girl
FRECKLES

Doreen Green isn't just a first-year computer science student: she secretly also has all the powers of both squirrel and girl! She uses her amazing abilities to fight crime **and** be as awesome as possible. You know her as...**The Unbeatable Squirrel Girl!** Let's catch up with what she's been up to until now, with...

Squirrel Girl *in a nutshell*

Squirrel Girl! @unbeatablesg
@xGALACTUSx hey dude thanks for not eating the planet after all!!

GALACTUS @xGALACTUSx
@unbeatablesg NO PROBLEM THAT PLANET OF NUTS YOU FOUND WAS WAY BETTER ANYWAY

Deadpool @pooltothedead
@unbeatablesg @xGALACTUSx Wait, what? You guys weren't joking about that?

Deadpool @pooltothedead
@unbeatablesg @xGALACTUSx Galactus ACTUALLY came to Earth?? Yesterday? The ACTUAL GALACTUS was HERE??

Deadpool @pooltothedead
@unbeatablesg @xGALACTUSx dang man I spent the whole day at home watching tv in my underpants

Deadpool @pooltothedead
@unbeatablesg @xGALACTUSx CALL ME NEXT TIME!!

Tony Stark @starkmantony
A bunch of my Iron Man suit parts showed up in NYC with moon dust on them. That's actually extremely valuable, so thanks @unbeatablesg.

Tippy-Toe @yoitstippytoe
@starkmantony CHITT CHUK CHITTT?

Tony Stark @starkmantony
@yoitstippytoe I can't understand you. None of my translation algorithms can understand you. Probably because you are a literal squirrel.

Tippy-Toe @yoitstippytoe
@starkmantony CHUKKA.... CHITT CHUK CHITTT?

Tony Stark @starkmantony
@unbeatablesg Little help?

Squirrel Girl! @unbeatablesg
@starkmantony she's asking you if you figured out that the dust came from the new moon restaurant

Tony Stark @starkmantony
@unbeatablesg @yoitstippytoe What new moon restaurant?

Tippy-Toe @yoitstippytoe
@starkmantony CHUTT CHUK CHUKK CHITTY CHIT

Squirrel Girl! @unbeatablesg
@starkmantony She says "The one that just opened up! The food's good, but it doesn't have much of an ATMOSPHERE"

Squirrel Girl! @unbeatablesg
@starkmantony hahaha, that's pretty good actually!! good work @yoitstippytoe

Tony Stark @starkmantony
@unbeatablesg @yoitstippytoe You guys know I'm the head of a major corporation, right?

Tony Stark @starkmantony
@unbeatablesg @yoitstippytoe I shouldn't even be hanging out here as it is

Nancy W. @sewwiththeflo
I bet being covered from head to toe in a living squirrel suit doesn't smell as bad as you think it would.

Nancy W. @sewwiththeflo
IMPORTANT UPDATE:

Nancy W. @sewwiththeflo
So it turns out being covered head to toe in a living squirrel suit doesn't smell as GOOD as you think it would either

search!

- #dinosaurs
- #basslass
- #clones
- #acronyms
- #nuthorde
- #TIPPPPPPPY!!

What, you think I won't fight a dinosaur? Are you crazy?
All I want to do is fight dinosaurs.
the unbeatable Squirrel Girl

One Hour Earlier...
In the Statue of Liberty's Head...
=sigh=
Still nobody, guys.
That's three hours we've been held hostage. Huh. I really thought we'd have been rescued by now.
Yo, who do you think's gonna save us?
Ooh, I hope Thor!
I love that woman. Abs of steel. Abs of the gods. And she hates it when people get taken hostage!
I hope Iron Man.
Yeah, except he just designed his armor to look like abs! They're painted on. Who does that?
Hello? He modeled the suit abs after his real abs.
Oh my gosh, can we please stop talking about abs?? Please let's talk about literally anything else.
Well, who do you think's gonna rescue us?
Oh, I don't think: I know. She's strong. She's smart.
She's the Unbeatable Squirrel Girl.

Could "She punches them until they stop doing crimes" be basically the perfect description of every super hero ever?
This author who just now wrote that sentence says: yes!

"...with a surprise."
ANOTHER STUPENDOUS SQUIRREL GIRL AND CAPTAIN AMERICA ADVENTURE...IN THE MERRY MARVEL FASHION!
FOR YEARS, YOU'VE MARVELED AS THE BRILLIANT SQUIRREL GIRL AND UNSTOPPABLE CAPTAIN AMERICA WORKED TOGETHER TO SAVE THE WORLD! BUT WHAT WAS THE FIRST TEAM-UP BETWEEN THESE TWO FANTASTIC FIGHTERS FOR FAIRNESS AND FREEDOM? AT LAST, THE STORY CAN FINALLY BE TOLD...A TALE SO DYNAMIC, SO EXCITING, SO FAR OUT THAT IT COULD ONLY BE CALLED...
MADNESS IN AMERICA!!
BUT CAPTAIN AMERICA! WHAT HAPPENED TO OUR PARTNERSHIP?
SORRY, SQUIRREL GIRL! BUT AS YOU CAN SEE...BASS LASS IS MY NEW PARTNER NOW!

Wait, wait!! Finish reading this comic before you run off to smash the state! There's a small chance that Captain America is wrong here!

Oh, to live in a world where *"Democracy seems pretty okay again, I guess"* is to Captain America as *"With great power comes great responsibility"* is to Spider-Man.

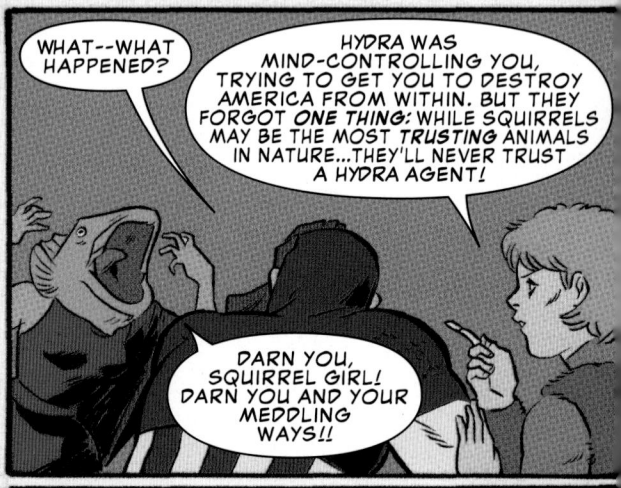

In that comic, Captain America says "Stand down! That's an order, Corporal," and then Corporal USA is all "Um yeah so the thing is, I think it's pretty clear we're both operating outside the traditional military chain of command here??"

If you get tired of literally all the money and want nations to start printing *more* money just to give it to you, open up an attraction where you get to wrestle the dinosaurs.

...a story that if I were to give it a title I believe I would be forced to call...

Hey, this reminds me: with great power doesn't come great responsibility! With great power *actually* comes great joules per second, or "watts," the integral of which over time measures the work performed. Librarians: please go ahead and file this comic in the "WOW! SCIENCE FACTS" section of the library.

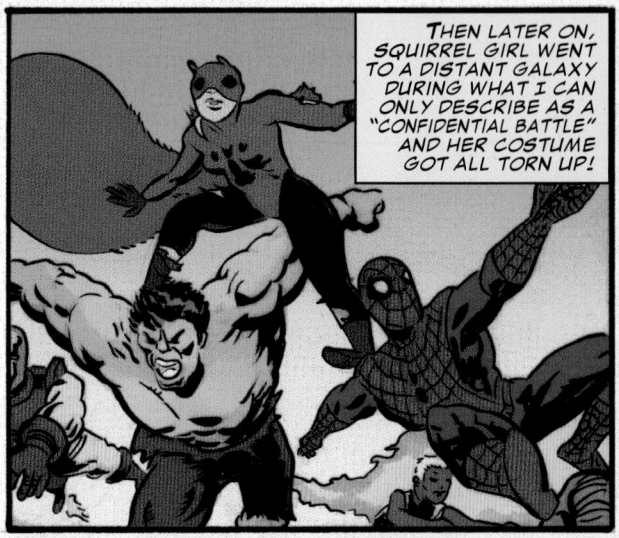

THAT COSTUME TURNED OUT TO BE A BAD GUY THOUGH, SO SHE GOT RID OF IT.

I JUST WANTED TO FIX MY TORN PANTS, AND NOW I HAVE TO DEAL WITH THIS BALONEY? WHY IS LAUNDRY SO HARD??

BLEH!!

WHY IS EVERYTHING ELSE SO HARD TOO, I MIGHT ADD??

Dude. I think you're thinking of Spider-Man.

Impossible! I--

WAIT, DOES SPIDER-MAN HAVE A TAIL? HE DOESN'T, DOES HE?

AW GEEZ, DID I TOTALLY JUST IMAGINE THIS BECAUSE HE'D OBVIOUSLY LOOK WAY BETTER WITH A TAIL??

Oh, right: spoiler alert for what happened to Spider-Man two decades ago! If you don't want to know what Spider-Man was doing two decades ago, please forget this page riiiight...now. Perfect!

Future Squirrel Girl's catch phrase isn't *"Let's get nuts,"* it's *"It's time to get nuts"* and the bad guys are always all, *"Okay, you're from the future, we get it"*.

Q: Who secret avenges the Secret Avengers? A: It's a secret. *Obviously.*

In case you were wondering, M.R. L.I.E.B.E.R.M.A.N. stands for *"Mechanical Resource For Locating Inefficiencies, Efficiencies, Battle-Exploitable Resources, and Machinery; Also Nuts."*

COME TO ME, MY SQUIRREL BRETHREN!!
CHHHHHHHHTTTTTTT
OH NO
GROSS
ERROR #8: CONFOUND THESE WRETCHED RODENTS
WHEN WILL YOU VILLAINS LEARN? YOU MESS WITH THE GIRL...
...THEN YOU GET THE SQUIRREL!!
WARNING: CURRENT BATTLE OUTPUT IS INSUFFICIENT TO DESTROY REMAINING 999,998 DOOMBOTS.
YOU MAY BE RIGHT. LOOKS LIKE WE'LL HAVE TO ENGAGE PLAN A.C.O.R.N.! M.R. L.I.E.B.E.R.M.A.N., RECALL ALL THE OTHER SQUIRREL GIRLS FROM THE TIMESTREAM!
ACKNOWLEDGED.
ZOOP
ARRR, I'LL BEAT THE BARNACLES OFF THESE BILGE RATS! HEAVE HO, ME HEARTIES!!
HARK! COULDE YE OLDE SQUIRRELLE GIRLLE BE OF ASSISTANCE??
THE MIGHT OF SQUIRREL GRRRL 2099 WILL END THIS RIGHT NOW!

And it's not even that weird, either. They should advertise it as one regular trick that sucks! Honestly, sometimes I wonder why I click on banner ads.

I've got squirrels. Lots of squirrels. Sometimes I count them just to make myself feel crazy.

I, uh, I just...read about Squirrel Girl on the Internet a lot, that's all! But on a better Internet than that kid has. I have access to Internet 2: Internet Platinum Supreme. Yeah: invite only. You've probably never heard of it.

Now let's go back to our shared dorm room, mysterious stranger!

Oh, by the way, you should know that we kinda told Squirrel Girl stories while we were waiting.

No way! Seriously? That's awesome! Did you tell them about my ***exploits?*** How I got Kraven to live in the ocean and beat Whiplash with my sweet ***electricity knowledge*** and then stopped ***Galactus*** on the ***moon*** with the power of ***friendship??***

No.

I don't think they would've believed me anyway.

Also, dude, you need to change your name to something like *"Squirrel Girl Who Is Not From The Future, Didn't Hang Around With Captain America in The '50s, Doesn't Tell Dad Jokes, And Doesn't Have Robot Duplicates, Also: Not Spider-Man."*

Whoa, robot duplicates? ***Dude.*** You have to tell me ***all about this.***

It sounds ***totally nuts!***

NEXT MONTH...

MORE AMAZING ADVENTURES WITH YOUR FAVORITE FANTASTIC HEROES!

♫ S.G.W.I.N.F.T.F.D.H.A.W.C.A.I.T.S.D.T.D.J.A.D.H.R.D.A.N.S.M., S.G.W.I.N.F.T.F.D.H.A.W.C.A.I.T.S.D.T.D.J.A.D.H.R.D.A.N.S.M., powers of both S.G.W.I.N.F.T.F.D.H.A.W.C.A.I.T.S.D.T.D.J.A.D.H.R.D.A.N.S.M. and girl. ♫

Letters From Nuts

Ryan!

Erica!

Send letters to mheroes@marvel.com or 135 W 50th St, 7th Floor, New York, NY 10020 (Please mark "OKAY TO PRINT")

Hope everyone enjoyed this issue! Our sincerest thanks/apologies to John Romita Sr., Jack Kirby, George Roussos, Dick Sprang, Edmond Hamilton, Todd McFarlane, Greg Wright, Mike Zeck, Christie Scheele, Chris Samnee, Matthew Wilson, Chris Giarrusso, Frank Miller and Lynn Varley for providing inspiration for the various "Squirrel Girl tails." Now on to your letters!

Congratulations on a tremendous first three issues of THE UNBEATABLE SQUIRREL GIRL! I am beyond pleased to see this comic and constantly amazed at how good it is. Like other commentators, I have largely abandoned other titles by the two big boys because everything out there seems bloated, grim, derivative, and tiresome. But Squirrel Girl has breathed new life into my pull list at my Friendly Local Comic Shop and I am exhausting the patience of my friends by telling them over and over again how they need to buy this book. Extra copies are being set aside as birthday and Christmas gifts. All I need now is an updated Heroclix figure so I can bring SG to tabletop gaming, a way to locate (and afford) all the wonderful alternate covers, and a Tippy-Toe bath toy. (To keep the Submariner from getting up to anything naughty.)

Excellent work, please continue until ALL evil has been vanquished from EVERY multiverse!

Best regards,
Kevin Hendryx
Austin, TX
WWSGD

RYAN: Thanks! Though as we have now had FOUR issues (well, now FIVE) since you wrote your letter, hopefully the next letter you write us won't be "the first three were great but then WHOAH, WHAT HAPPENED??" (please do not write this letter). And my favorite thing to say (well, about comics) is that it's a medium, not a genre, and that there's room enough for all sorts of stories here. So let's tell all sorts of stories!

p.s.: WWSGD? CLEARLY she would eat nuts and/or kick butts.

ERICA: AH! Such kind words! It warms my heart. I love having a diversity of stories to pick from and I think we're starting to get more of that at the forefront now. My own comic collection spans titles from Uncle Scrooge to Sky Doll. But honestly we're not trying to do something different, we're just doing something that we'd want to read ourselves.

I absolutely adore Squirrel Girl. She is my favorite super hero of all time in the history of ever. I recommend this comic to everybody I know who is into comics. And I'm really thankful my brother showed me this book. I find her a very relatable character and I love the humor in the comics. I also appreciate that she isn't like any other comic book character I've come across and the comic is something anybody can enjoy. Keep up the amazing work you guys are doing! Also when decorating Easter eggs this year I made Doreen Green/ Squirrel Girl and Tippy Toe themed Easter eggs so I've attached a picture for you guys.

Susie S.

RYAN: Awesome! I love when people hear about comics by someone sharing their issue, because I feel like comics live when they're shared around and not stuffed in a bag and put into a box. Thank you for the kind words, and thank your brother for me too! And those eggs are off the HOOK.

Dear purveyors of fine squirrel literature,

I've never written into a comic before, I don't even read comics very often, but after arriving at the store too early... and then too late, I finally got copies of Squirrel Girl and felt like I had to thank you!

I followed Squirrel Girl during her time in the GLA, and I am ecstatic to see her headlining her own title. I've never really felt a strong connection to any heroes in the past, but I can really relate to Squirrel Girl, she just feels down to earth. On top of the excellent writing and characterization, the art is just adorable. Congratulations on a great release, I don't even have any questions (unless you can suggest a good one), I just wanted to say thanks for getting me interested in comics for the first time in years.

Thanks,
Robert 'MrAptronym'

RYAN: Thanks, Robert! And let me suggest a question for you: "How come Doreen hasn't met any flying squirrels yet?" And the answer is that, until LITERALLY YESTERDAY when Erica proved me wrong, I thought that there weren't any in North America. I saw some flying squirrels at a zoo when I was a kid and I guess I assumed all zoo animals were from far away? Anyway, turns out they DO live on at least the same continent that Doreen lives on, so I'm a big dummy but at least I'm slightly smarter now, and we'll hopefully see some in the comic sooner rather than later.

ERICA: The 44 varieties of flying squirrel live in North America, Europe, and Asia, but there's like one kind in America and one that spans from Finland to Japan and then the other 42 are all in Asia. So, really Asia is still has the best flying-squirrel-to-continent ratio. Oh, wait, the original question wasn't about flying squirrels. I'm glad you like our take on Doreen, being a long time Squirrel Girl fan!

Dear Ryan & Erica,

What's with all this talk of Chipmunk Hunk? Are you teasing us with a prospective Woodland Avengers? I could definitely get behind that series.

Keep up the good work,
Mitch

RYAN: I wasn't planning the Woodland Avengers, but now that you mention it it's all I can think about, so let's say... DEFINITELY YES, THAT IS EXACTLY WHAT IS GOING TO HAPPEN.

ERICA: I thought we weren't supposed to talk about the Yosemite Avengers until after Secret Wars.

Dear Ryan & Erica,

Thank you for teaming up an empowered girl with the world's most charismatic microfauna. You have made a lot of female squirrel biologists very happy. (By "a lot," I mean proportionally... sadly, we aren't that numerous.) I especially appreciate Doreen's sensible footwear choice and her blind optimism about the coolness of squirrels. Please keep making this comic FOREVER. Also, if you can swing it, please introduce a paleontologist who is woefully dull compared to Squirrel Girl. For an added touch of realism. My boyfriend studies theropods, and I'm sure I don't have to say who's the bigger hit at parties.

Lastly, please enjoy this portrait of me with some of my squirrel friends. I would have also included a photo of my pre-Unbeatable Squirrel Girl costume, but the furry one-piece bathing suit is, erm, a little alarming.

Sincerely
Amanda

RYAN: Amanda! I didn't even NOTICE the squirrels at first because they match your whole ensemble so well! I had never considered using baby squirrels as a fashion accessory until now but clearly I was not dreaming big enough. That is an amazing picture. I love it.

As someone who was always big into theropods from my Dinosaur Comics strip and who is now big into squirrels for obvious reasons, I feel like I can't decide who is cooler between you and your boyfriend! Probably you're both tied for first? But in any case I feel like you and your boyfriend and I could share some pretty friggin' scintillating conversation at cool parties, so please attend some cool parties soon and invite me, THANKS IN ADVANCE.

ERICA: I think I know who the winner is, because I'm pretty sure small mammals made it past the KT extinction. Amanda, I am 100% jealous of your woodland creature friends. So many of us watched Sleeping Beauty (and should totally watch it again because of that Eyvind Earle art) and said, "yes, when I grow up, I'm going to have a woodland posse" but we gave up and moved onto other, lesser endeavors. I salute you.

Next: HIPPO FIIIIIIIIIIIGHT!

WHO WILL BE THE NEWEST FRIENDS OF the unbeatable Squirrel Girl ?!

PICK TWO!

(Answer Inside)

Doreen Green isn't just a first-year computer science student: she secretly also has all the powers of both squirrel and girl. She uses her amazing abilities to fight crime **and** be as awesome as possible. You know her as...**The Unbeatable Squirrel Girl**. Let's catch up with what she's been up to until now, with...

Squirrel Girl *in a nutshell*

Squirrel Girl! @unbeatablesg
RT if you helped defeat Mysterion and his ROBOT DINOSAURS and saved the statue of liberty!!

Squirrel Girl! @unbeatablesg
RT @unbeatablesg: RT if you helped defeat Mysterion and his ROBOT DINOSAURS and saved the statue of liberty!!

Squirrel Girl! @unbeatablesg
Yes I did just retweet myself

Squirrel Girl! @unbeatablesg
PROBABLY because I totally just helped defeat Mysterion and his ROBOT DINOSAURS and saved the STATUE OF LIBERTY??

Squirrel Girl! @unbeatablesg
@HULKYSMASHY hey thanks for the RT!

HULK @HULKYSMASHY
@unbeatablesg HULK SMASH PUNY DINOSAUR!!

Squirrel Girl! @unbeatablesg
@HULKYSMASHY haha we sure did!!

HULK @HULKYSMASHY
@unbeatablesg HULK GLAD WHEN SOCIOLOGICAL PROBLEMS CAN BE SOLVED BY SMASHING

Squirrel Girl! @unbeatablesg
@HULKYSMASHY yeah it's always nice when things work out that way actually

CAMPUS BANK

CampusBank @campusbank
Good news! We've fixed the giant squirrel-suit-shaped hole in our wall. CampusBank: We've Got Class Too™.

Squirrel Girl! @unbeatablesg
@campusbank okay but let's not forget the only reason that hole is there is because i saved all the hostages

CAMPUS BANK

CampusBank @campusbank
We think you'll be INTERESTed in our new savings account fee schedules. CampusBank: We've Got Class Too™.

Squirrel Girl! @unbeatablesg
@campusbank cool pun bro but can we at least acknowledge how i saved all the hostages

CAMPUS BANK

CampusBank @campusbank
We can't take all the CREDIT for our new student charge card plans. CampusBank: We've Got Class Too™.

Squirrel Girl! @unbeatablesg
@campusbank sometimes i wonder why i follow so many #brands on social media

Squirrel Girl! @unbeatablesg
Okay everyone, HONESTLY, tell me this wall doesn't look WAY BETTER with a hole:

search!

#hippothehippo

#imwithskrull

#liontomeetyou

#squirrelgirl

#kicksbuttseatsnuts

Oh that poor narrator

Oh well! There go all our plans for our spin-off comic: The Unbeatable Squirrel Scouts And Their Warm And Soft, Yet Also Furry, Battle Suits.

Attention, everyone who knows a Mrs. Fluffy Lumpkins in real life: yes, she absolutely *would* want to hear about this comic page! Even if you haven't spoken to her in years! *Especially* if you haven't spoken to her in years!

We don't even eat marbles! We've never eaten marbles!! Who designs these games?

Plus a lot of the other heroes don't really talk as much as I do. I dunno. I don't want to make it weird for them, but then I worry it's weird to *not* introduce myself, you know?

I like the idea of eating so much that the most important thing about your food isn't *what* you eat, but rather just the number of pounds it weighs. I--I really like eating, you guys.

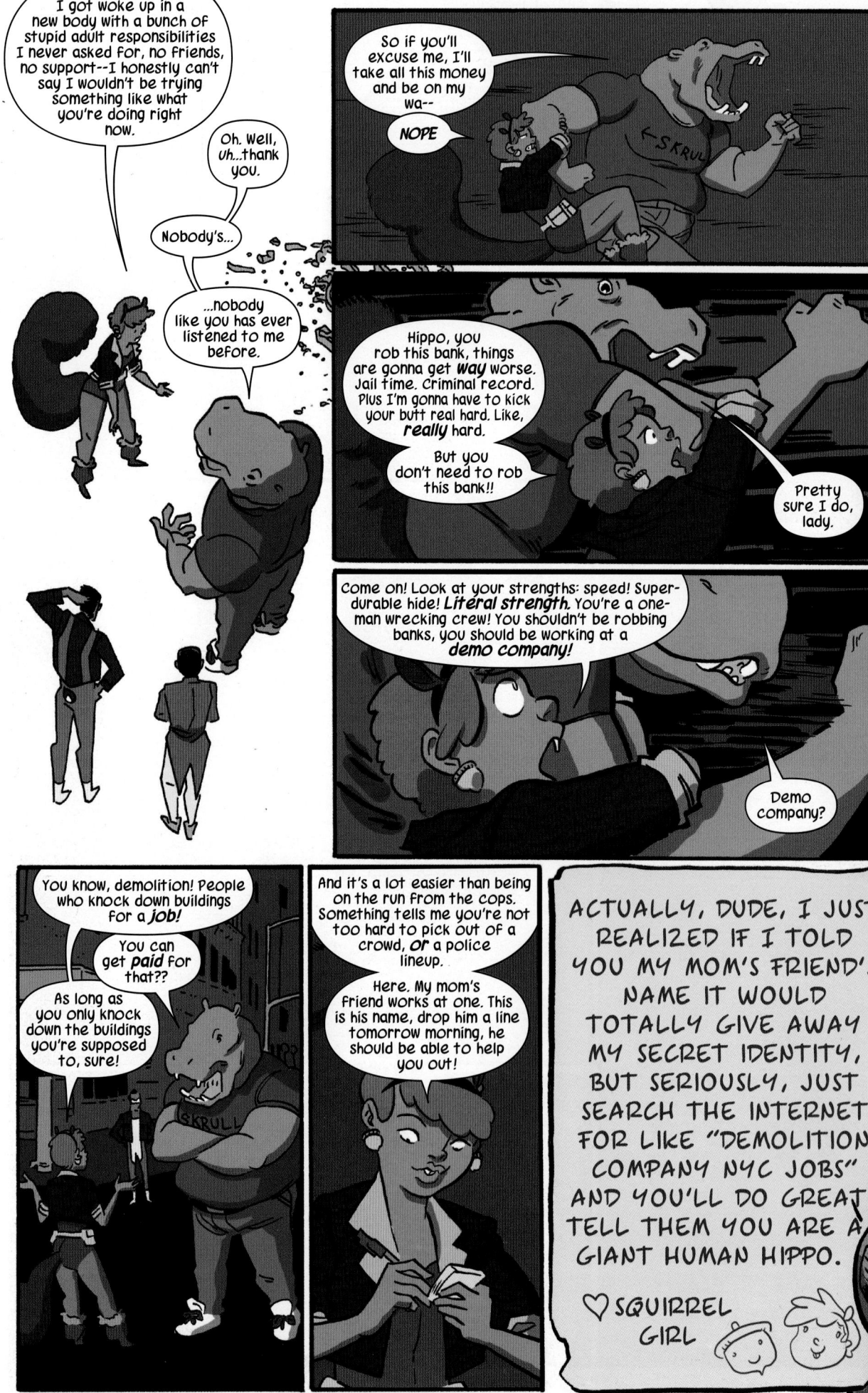

The demolition company Squirrel Girl's mom's friend works at is called *"Yo, What's Up, We Hate Buildings Too"* because who wouldn't hire a demo company with that name? The answer: nobody.

Okay, I promise that with Squirrel Girl, Koi Boi, Chipmunk Hunk, and Bass Lass, we are done with animal rhyming names. *Promise.* For at least the next eleven pages.

This flashback is from our first issue, and if you haven't bought it yet, good news: holding out for six months just got you ***two*** panels from it for free! At this rate you'll be able to read the whole first issue in several dozen years!

Does every story ever need a *friendship montage?* The answer: absolutely, unambiguously, unequivocally yes. It would improve any story; there can be no argument.

hey there monkey if you can understand me loudly screech once for yes and like fifteen times in a row for no

Okay, secretly the monkeys have taught themselves some sign language but that's *it*.

See, this is exactly why zoo regulations ***clearly*** state to close all lion doors ***before*** having a medical emergency.

Doreen, has this truly been the most pointless visit to the zoo?
The fact that today I've either beaten or played to death "Knitting Simulator 3000," "Super Cat Trivia II Turbo" and "Choleric, Frustrated Birds" says: yes!
Uh... dad??
POW
One sec, I just need to get my costu--
...huh?
SWOOOOOSH
Oh crap oh crap oh crap.
Oh crap.
One of yours?
I--
I--

I'm not familiar with the type of thing I'm seeing.
Remain calm, citizens. I'll handle this!

Also: "who," "how," and "why." And a few more "whats" for good measure.

I don't know who this Chuck X. Avier guy is, but he sure likes talking up this School For Gifted Youngsters! Weird!!

She should stop even if her hat is cute. Even if her hat is basically the cutest, that only gets her so far, okay??

Chit chitttt chiiiiiitt
Wait, I can translate this! Okay, so what she's saying is basically "She's just pretending to like you. All your friends are. They think it's funny. They're not wrong."
Wait, what?
Then there's something about...about how "they need to pay"?
What the--?
SWOOOOOSH
SWOOOOOSH
SWOOOOOSH
SWOOOOOSH
Chhht chut chuttt
Hey, this is Peter Parker's place! He's Spider-Man, but don't tell anyone!!
Cheett chitt chitty
And hooray! Here Girl Squirrel's actually talking about the Golden Rule! That's where you do unto others as you'd have them do unto--
Wait.
Cheeeeeeeeeett
Wait, no, she's telling him to follow the Iron Rule: do unto others before they can do unto you first. And now she's on about...about "demanding respect"?
Aw geez.
Chitt
Chitt
Chitt
Listen, I got into the narration business because all I ever wanted to do was tell people where things were taking place, and how much later those things were from the last things they saw taking place! That page earlier where it was "20 Minutes Later" every panel? Bliss.
That was great.
But what Girl Squirrel is saying here is actually super awful, so y'all can find someone else to narrate the rest of this issue, because I am out!!
I don't even want to say what she's saying here. It's awful, all about how everyone else wants to hurt him.
And he should "hurt them first"?
Girl Squirrel, nooooooo!
Chitt
Chitt
Chitt

SKREEECH!!
Oh, you stupid ca---
Mew?
Mew, it's 6:30 in the morning.
What's the matter, Bunbun? What's got you upset, hmm?
Not chatty, huh?
It's too bad you can't talk, Mew.
Man.
I gotta meet someone named "Cat Brat."

CONTINUED NEXT MONTH!

Okay I'm back, but only to say that Cat Brat sounds awesome and I want to narrate their comic instead. *Peace.*

Dear Squirrel Girl Editor,

What in the H-E-single Asgardian hockey stick is the matter with you?! I have just read the advance copy of SQUIRREL GIRL #4!!! ONE PAGE?!! SQUIRREL GIRL DEFEATS GALACTUS IN ONE PAGE?!!! Thank you, jerk-faces. Thank you for ruining Marvel Comics for all time!

The Marvel that *I* knew, the Marvel that *I* grew up with made sense! LOGICAL sense! Armor was transistor powered! Steve Rogers could hide his shield under his jacket! And NOBODY could beat Galactus! NO ONE!

Yes, it's canon that Squirrel Girl's defeated Doctor Doom, M.O.D.O.K., and even Fin Fang Foom, but none of those guys are the Mighty Galactus! Silver Surfer just fought Galactus for three straight issues--that's 59 more pages than shown here--and the Surfer STILL LOST! Now THAT'S a Galactus story that makes SENSE! (And on sale soon as part of the SILVER SURFER: WORLDS APART trade paperback.) And now you've gone and defeated him in what is tantamount to ONE PANEL?! And by someone with SQUIRREL POWERS?!

NUTS TO YOU, PAL! NUTS! TO! YOU!

Dan Slott
3 Doors Down
Marvel Entertainment, NY

RYAN: Hey Dan! Nice to hear from you, buddy! I was stoked to run your great quote on the cover of our issue #2 ("I can't recommend the new SQUIRREL GIRL book enough! It's NUTS!") but I think you may have overlooked something because there's not much here I can use. The best I've come up with from your letter is, "I have just read... Squirrel Girl #4!!!... Now THAT'S a Galactus story! ...SQUIRREL POWERS... TO YOU, PAL!" which is actually a pretty great quote after all, so-thanks!

ERICA: Dan, calm down.

Dear Ryan and Erica,

I just wanted to let you know how much I've been enjoying THE UNBEATABLE SQUIRREL GIRL thus far. An encounter with Galactus so early in the series would seem difficult to pull off successfully, but I thought it was handled very well. The way Squirrel Girl hears Galactus's words not just in her own language, but her own vernacular, was a nice touch. The full page of an American teenage girl sitting on the giant shoulder of a god-like being older than the universe, together contemplating the Earth set against the background of the cosmos, is perhaps Erica's most beautiful image.

I also noticed that your Galactus story parallels that of the original Galactus trilogy by Lee and Kirby, which I am old enough to have read when it first appeared. In both cases, the encounter with Galactus commences hot on the heels of another adventure and ends with the characters resuming their everyday lives. I'll certainly be looking forward to future installments.

Make Mine Marvel!
Charles Hoffman,
Van Nuys, CA

P.S. I've taken the liberty of attaching a picture of myself with Erica's father, Red Hook, 1980s. I know that he would be delighted with Squirrel Girl.

RYAN: I didn't even see these parallels until you pointed them out, but now I'm happy they're there!

ERICA: Oh wow. That's an old photo. That's possibly a pre-Erica photo. Anyway, I think Galactus had to be in the first arc. Dan Slott's work on the character really established who the character is after her initial appearance in Marvel Super-Heroes Winter Special, and more importantly established that she wins fights against the toughest of the tough. After pitting her against some of Marvel's biggest baddies (Giganto, Fin Fang Foom, Thanos) it only makes sense that we start off by going one further and putting her up against Marvel's biggest (literally?) baddie.

Dear Unbeatable Squirrel-team,

As a long time comic reader and Marvel fan, I want to thank you for one of, heck, THE most brilliantly executed, on-point character portrayals in issue #4.

Only SQUIRREL GIRL could leave me satisfied with a one-page comic. Sometimes nothing more needs to be said, and you said it perfectly.

I also appreciate the interaction with the fans you guys show in the responses of your letter columns, showing that you care about us as much as we care about you. The SG fans may not be as garishly loud as those of a certain Spider-Man, but like the squirrels, we are there, hiding in the trees and eating nuts.

Squirrel Girl may not be as widely known of a hero, she's not in it for the flash and publicity. She's the hero we need, there to do things right and put a smile on our faces. Heck, I bet not even Howard the Duck, among the grumpiest, most perennially frustrated and disappointed of heroes, could resist cracking a smile in her presence.

Now if you'll excuse me, I've just finished up the letters column and am off to see if the tiny print continues on the blank pages to follow...wait...what's this? BONUS COMIC!

You guys (for lack of a proper gender-neutral pronoun) rock!

Nathan

RYAN: I appreciate you taking the time to write a letter only three pages into the comic! I kinda wish all letters were like that, all "Dear Squirrel Girl people, I can't wait to see what happens next! I guess I'm about to now though! Well, bye!"

ERICA: I personally enjoy "dude" as a gender-neutral term. It's often thought of as male, but it just means individual. Before the 60s (which is when it started to be misused as "man") it meant either a city slicker or someone who is very fashion forward and that's definitely us. 100%.

P.S. I'm glad you like SQUIRREL GIRL!

Hello again, lovely people, and thank you again for the brilliance that is SQUIRREL GIRL! I have just finished #4... And you have to make SQUIRREL GIRL spin-offs! "Squirrel Girl, Herald of Galactus" has to be a thing! What must we do to make

it happen?! On the subject, how about a Magneto/Squirrel-Girl eighteen-chapter epic that dwarfs all those 90's crossovers that we all remember so fondly?

No? Okay...what about "Squirrel Girl's Adventures In Babysitting" filling in all the gaps where SG had to stay home and look after Luke Cage's kid?

SQUIRREL GIRL is easily my favorite comic book to date, across all publishers and genres. Thank you again for everything!

Tim P.
Plymouth, England

RYAN: I keep thinking of how Magneto and Squirrel Girl would get along. He's such a serious, dour guy! Maybe they should go on a road trip together. Maybe... maybe they should DEFINITELY go on a road trip together.

I wanted to write in to complain that my copy of UNBEATABLE SQUIRREL GIRL #4 must have been a counterfeit. The bottom of the first page clearly states that all of the pages following the letters page would be blank. I was deeply disappointed to find all sorts of art, words, and story along with ZERO blank pages! Either it was counterfeit or someone in quality control needs to be fired!

Seriously though, it was one of the most entertaining comics I've read in some time. I can't remember the last time I've started laughing uproariously and had to catch my breath and re-read what I had just read to make sure I got it all... And this happened several times during this issue. If the rest of the pages HAD been blank it would have been an amazing gag of its own. Great stuff!

Sean Bayless

RYAN: Sean, the truth of the matter is that after printing the blank pages we felt bad about maybe ripping people off, so we requested the staff at your (and everyone's!) local comic book store to create and draw in their own conclusion to the story on the remaining blank pages, so everyone got their own different ending! I'm glad you liked yours! P.S.: Let me know what some of the jokes were, so I can use them in future issues.

ERICA: I'm going to respond to the second half of your letter since Ryan responded to the first half. I was reading this script while my boyfriend was in the other end of the apartment and he kept walking over to find out what I was laughing at. This also happens a lot when I'm out working with Joe Quinones (artist on HOWARD THE DUCK) and we'll chuckle to ourselves about the pages we're working on while in a cafe. So you are not alone in this.

Congratulations, Ryan and Erica, on creating a fun and entertaining comic. After reading the first issue of this comic, I found myself already going nuts for this series. I love that Doreen is just as awkward and silly as any other person. Also, it's pretty cool that she "defeats" these baddies just by being nice and friendly to them. I'm definitely looking forward to many more issues to come!

The photo attached is me with a baby squirrel that my family cared for recently. He's now living with 12 other little squirrels at our local wildlife rescue!

Kevin Krause

RYAN: Thanks! Also when I started this comic I honestly did not expect there would be so many people with squirrels in their lives. I did not expect our letters column would be mostly photos of people with squirrels on them. I'm happy this turned out to be the case!

ERICA: This is worth it just for all the pictures of wee baby squirrels people send us.

I've seriously never written to a comic book before. (It seemed silly.) But I had to let you all know that THE UNBEATABLE SQUIRREL GIRL is my new most favorite thing. Ever. I love it. I love it. I love it.

Jesse

P.S. Please tell me there's some sweet Squirrel Girl merch in the works? I would love to buy me some Doreen Green action figures, buttons, etc.

RYAN: Jesse, I would love some Squirrel Girl action figures! We don't get to tell the merchandise companies what to make, but now I will absolutely tell the merchandise companies what to make: a Squirrel Girl action figure with at least 12 points of articulation, and which comes packaged with a Tippy-Toe figure that can lock onto her shoulder and a randomly selected Deadpool card. I've got the designs right here. Call me, merchandise companies.

ERICA: I want a Squirrel Girl toy so bad. In the meantime I've just been collecting squirrel paraphernalia. Right now I'm up to two necklaces, a purse and a stuffed animal.

Rico did design six different Squirrel Girl buttons for the release of the book though. He's way more on top of this merchandising stuff than we are. Have you seen all the Spider-Gwen stuff he's put together? YOW!

To the gloriously deranged minds behind SQUIRREL GIRL:

Kudos! Amazing work! I've been hooked since the first issue! I have but one humble question. When do we get to meet The Chipmunk Hunk? Convention season is upon us and I need to know what my cosplay should look like.

Keep up the fabulous work, Doreen is a gem and I haven't laughed so much in ages

Josh W

RYAN: Hey thanks, Josh! As for meeting Chipmunk Hunk, I can't say for sure when we'll be seeing him! If that bothers you, I guess that's just the NEXT ISSUE you need to deal with. It's probably ISSUE #6 on your list.

Oh wait, never mind, this is issue six already. He's in this issue, surprise!!

ERICA: OH GOD I'M SO EXCITED FOR CHIPMUNK HUNK COSPLAY. I NEVER CONSIDERED THAT MIGHT BE A POSSIBILITY. YOU'D BETTER SEND US PHOTOS.

Next: Avengers Assemble?

On Sale 7/1/15!

Attention Squirrel Scouts! Make sure to check out our production blog, **unbeatablesquirrelgirl.tumblr.com**, where we post behind-the-scenes stuff on how the book gets made, along with all sorts of cool things *you* make: fanart, cosplay, whatever!

the unbeatable Squirrel Girl
EH! 2015

Doreen Green isn't just a first-year computer science student: she secretly also has all the powers of both squirrel and girl. She uses her amazing abilities to fight crime **and** be as awesome as possible. You know her as...**The Unbeatable Squirrel Girl.** Let's catch up with what she's been up to until now, with...

Squirrel Girl *in a nutshell*

Squirrel Girl! @unbeatablesg
PUBLIC SERVICE ANNOUNCEMENT: Everyone should go to the zoo and talk to every animal there. Just go and chat up every animal!

Squirrel Girl! @unbeatablesg
Because how do you know you CAN'T talk to animals unless you've tried with every animal?? And they've got lots of animals there!

Squirrel Girl! @unbeatablesg
Also yes I am aware that there are elements of zoos that are NOT UNPROBLEMATIC but where else are you gonna chat up mad lemurs

Squirrel Girl! @unbeatablesg
Besides Madagascar I mean

Tippy-Toe @yoitstippytoe
@unbeatablesg CHITTT CHITTY CHIT CHIT

Squirrel Girl! @unbeatablesg
@yoitstippytoe dude, I meant "mad lemurs" in the "lots of lemurs" sense, not that they're angry! The zoo ones were actually mostly sleepy

Squirrel Girl! @unbeatablesg
@yoitstippytoe lots of sleepy lemurs to be had at your local zoo, visit today

Nancy W. @sewwiththeflo
I was at the zoo yesterday when the lions got out and this "Girl Squirrel" saved everyone.

Nancy W. @sewwiththeflo
As near as I can tell she is a squirrel with the INVERSE proportional strength of a girl? Or something?

Nancy W. @sewwiththeflo
What even is biology, you guys.

Nancy W. @sewwiththeflo
How do bodies even work.

Nancy W. @sewwiththeflo
Local woman publicly questions how a squirrel can have the powers of a girl. Vets hate me.

Tony Stark @starkmantony
@unbeatablesg Getting reports of fights breaking out all over NYC. Can I assume you are on this?

Squirrel Girl! @unbeatablesg
@starkmantony uh can you assume it's like 6:30am here and i just woke up

Tony Stark @starkmantony
@unbeatablesg My post woke you up? Huh. You have a special notification sound for me, don't you.

Squirrel Girl! @unbeatablesg
@starkmantony um, YEAH, it's your old 60s-style PERSONAL JINGLE that you hoped we'd all just forgot about and it's AMAZING

Squirrel Girl! @unbeatablesg
@starkmantony ♫ Tony Stark / Makes you feel / He's the cool exec / With a heart of steel ♫

Tony Stark @starkmantony
@unbeatablesg Hold on a second.

Tony Stark @starkmantony
@unbeatablesg I just remotely erased that song from your phone and from every other mirror online.

Squirrel Girl! @unbeatablesg
@starkmantony ♫ Tony Stark / Makes me feel / That I'm super glad / That I backed up that song to a device not connected to the internet ♫

Squirrel Girl! @unbeatablesg
Hey I dunno if any criminals follow me but JUST IN CASE, you should know that KOI BOI and CHIPMUNK HUNK are fighting crime now too!

Squirrel Girl! @unbeatablesg
Also if you are a criminal please stop doing crimes. #crimeadvice

search!

- #databasesoneohone
- #databasesoneohFUN
- #dontthrowshadeonmyfriends
- #breakfastbeats
- #boythor
- Bostonian Cameos

All these database facts are true, by the way. So now you can impress all your friends with your college-level knowledge of database design, so long as they don't ask a single follow-up question!

Seriously, you know so much about databases now! You can now officially go to a party where you don't know anyone and pass yourself off as a database engineer. In fact, surprise, ***this is now mandatory.***

I believe this is the world's first database model riot. UPDATE database_riots SET status='awesome'??

"Stop rioting or we'll punch you" is up there with "Stop eating or we'll feed you" on the List of Lines That, You Know, Probably Won't Work As Well As You Expected.

Ratatoskr

From Wikipedia. You can tell because this looks a lot like a Wikipedia entry.

In Norse mythology, **Ratatoskr** (Old Norse, generally considered to mean "drill-tooth"[1] or "bore-tooth"[2]) is a talking god-squirrel who runs up and down the world tree Yggdrasil. There are several tales of Ratatoskr provoking with slanderous gossip[3]. Ratatoskr is attested in both the Poetic Edda and the Prose Edda. Scholars have proposed theories about the implications of the squirrel.

Contents [hide]

1 Etymology
2 Attestations
3 Theories
4 Notes
5 Asgardian Responses
6 References
7 External links

Also, she was ripping off my name the whole time and that was annoying. There. I said it.

Should we change the name of our comic from "The Unbeatable Squirrel Girl" to "Hi We're A Bunch of CS Students Who Read A Wikipedia Page"?
Market research says: "hah hah hah nope"

We'd smash our way in through the windows, but Tony installed better glass after I, *uh*, liberated some of his suits earlier. And can I just say: *Classic Tony.*

Sometimes I talk about things being nuts, okay? It happens, and *we all just have to deal with it.*

Listen, we have reason to believe an evil super squirrel from history but also from space is behind everyone wanting to fight each other, including you guys, so I need to you all to calm down, let me know where Thor is, and then--
Oooh, the Squirrel Lady thinks squirrels are the criminal masterminds here.
Big surprise, right??
Let me guess, now only you can save the day.
That's really convenient for her, isn't it? Real convenient.
Hey Squirrel Girl, who are your friends? The Mixed Nuts?
Okay, I'm gonna let those slide because I know you're not being yourselves right now, but if we could all stop fighting for a moment, I would actually like you to meet my friends so then we can all solve this problem together.
This is Tippy-Toe and she's my best squirrel friend, this is Chipmunk Hunk and he can talk to chipmunks, this is Koi Boi and he can talk to fish, and this is Nancy and she's my roommate and she's awesome and we're best human friends and I love her.
Hey.
chitt
And I warn you: if you can't say anything nice, don't say anything at all.
I--

26 Seconds Later...
Doreen, you didn't have to--
Hello?! They were the ones being jerks.

Captain America doesn't have a lock screen on his phone because who is gonna steal it from him? Seriously. Um, besides our heroes in this book, I mean.

TRUE MARVEL COMICS FACTS: "Oh Frigga!" is the lady version of "By Odin's beard." Tell your friends! It's definitely a fact!!

See, Thor, ***this*** is why I keep saying you should contribute to Wikipedia. This is ***way*** more useful than their summary. *Sheesh!*

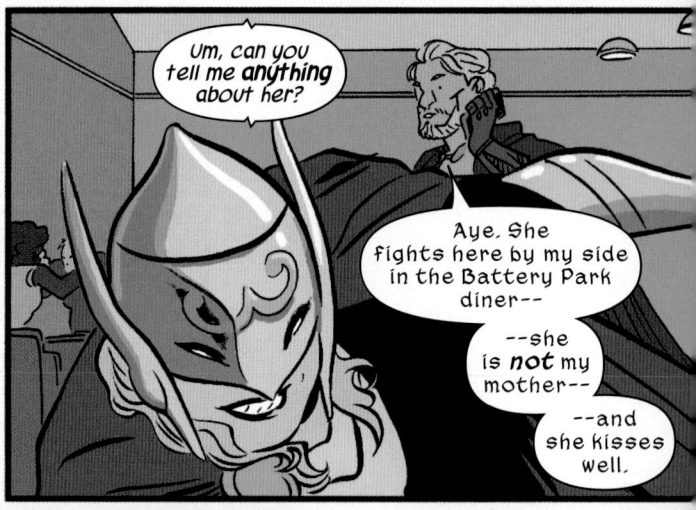

You can read *Thor #4* to see the one time they smooched if you want! But be warned: If you do, we'll all know you're someone who reads comics just to Flip Forward to the smooches. ***We'll all know. Even your parents will know.***

TRUE REAL WORLD FACTS: Did you know that the side of a hammer is called the *"cheek"*? And the part you hit with is called the *"face,"* which is attached to the *"neck."* Hammers are these adorable little metal heads we invented to solve our problems.

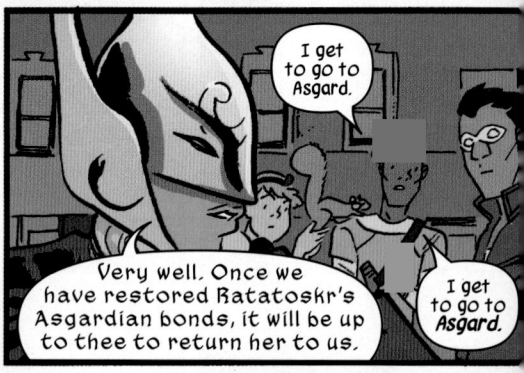

Oh, I forgot to mention! That duck on the last page? His name is Chip Zducksky, and he's off to have his own adventures that we, for reasons of good taste, cannot publish here. Fare thee well, Chip Zducksky!

Seriously, I don't know if you realize this, but what you're saying really makes it sound like you actually did it and you're just toying with u--OHHHH.

Come on. Do you really think I'm going to give everyone the hope of a better, more wonderful world--a world where even our pets have superpowers and can talk--simply so I can pull it away again and make you all look like idiots?

Like complete and total idiots?
Just because you're all so easy to manipulate by being so petty and jealous and afraid all the time, you think I'm the real Kataroskr??

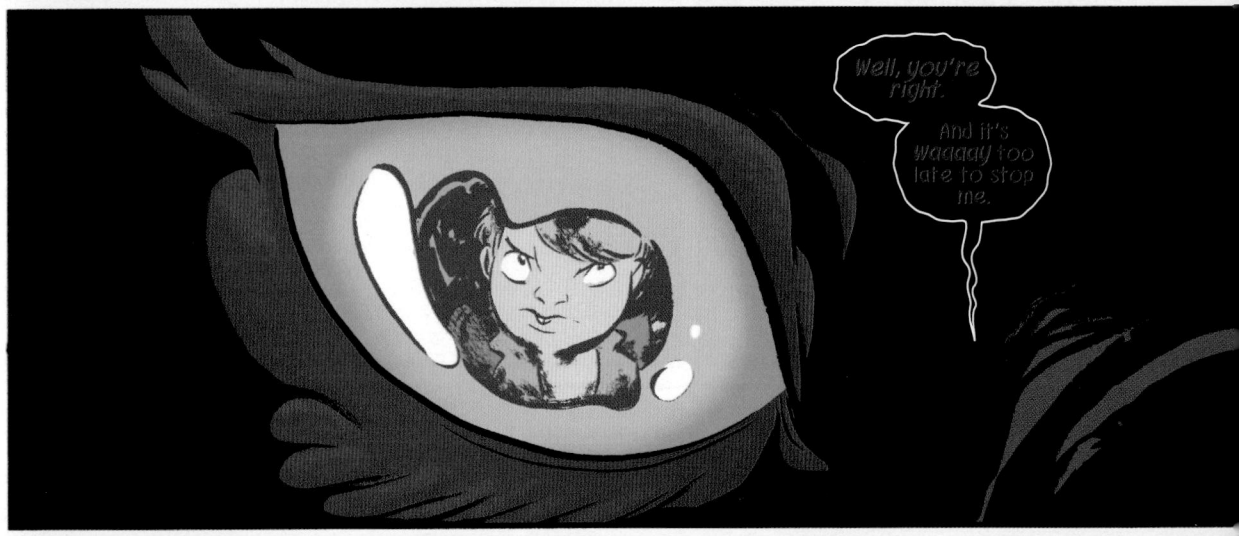
Well, you're right.
And it's waaaay too late to stop me.

Says you, jerk! Squirrels: attack!!
Chipmunks: attack!!
Koi: stand ready for when we knock her into the water!!

TRUE MARVEL COMICS FACTS: what Ratatoskr says there is *so unkind,* the only way we could print it was by making sure it wasn't in English! So yeah, I guess just make sure you don't show this comic to any squirrels you want to be friends with.

Look, I get why you're fighting me. I do, but you need to understand.
The only reason I'm ending your world is to make room for something better.
Death's a part of life, you know?
Like death from old age, maybe, and even that sucks!
Grow up. You gotta clear out the deadwood sometimes, otherwise we'd all still be running around with dinosaurs.
And that would've been amazing!
Stop trying to talk up death, you jerk!!
Your kind never listens. Now you and your little friends are gonna attack me, right?
We're not just going to attack you, scum. We're going to take you down.
Yeah. Looks like we just got promoted to Animal Control.
And you're overdue for a shot!
With fists!!
In the arm!
Gah!!
SWAT
The End.
Just kidding!
This is obviously not The End.
But you do have to wait a month until the actual end though.
Sorry!!
It's just, it's gonna take us at least a month to figure out how Squirrel Girl gets out of this one!

Send letters to mheroes@marvel.com or 135 W 50th St, 7th Floor, New York, NY 10020 (Please mark "OKAY TO PRINT")

Dear Erica and Ryan,

Could you please make a spin off series for Squirrel Grrrl 2099. She looks badasssss! Power of squirrels and lazerss!

Thanks
Brent, Auckland, NZ

RYAN: I'm actually way more interested in what Bass Lass (and Squirrel Earl) are up to! What are her powers? Does wearing a fish head and an evening gown give her powers, and if so, how did she ever discover that? Would - would I get her powers under similar circumstances?

ERICA: I'm torn on this. On the one hand, I prefer to have something like that not get any bigger than it is because we all have our own expectations of who she is and defining it would narrow down who she is. On the other hand, earlier this year, my boyfriend read Doom 2099 out loud to me as we lay on the sofa so I'm definitely into some 2099 craziness.

Hey!

First of all, this is not my email account. I am only 9. This is my mom's account. Second of all, I know I'm a little young to be reading SQUIRREL GIRL, but I am addicted to any girl super hero comic. Third of all, you are awesome, period. Here are my top 5 comic books (not in any type of order):

- Ms. Marvel
- Squirrel Girl
- Supergirl
- Wonder Woman
- Buffy Vampire Slayer

Can't wait to read more comics.

Eliot P.

RYAN: Hey Eliot, thanks! That's great company to be in. This was a very sweet letter, and I'm stoked you like so many female super heroes! There's a whole universe of them out there, and it's getting bigger all the time. Hooray!

ERICA: I think as long as you can open up Unbeatable Squirrel Girl and know what the words mean, you're old enough to read it. Ryan's right (don't tell him I said that), there are a ton of great books out there. When you're a couple of years older, e-mail again and I'll have a giant list of recommendations.

For the Avengers premiere, as a fundraiser, my manager agreed to dress up as any super hero his reports wanted as long as we each donated $100 to charity. We all chipped in and after a brief discussion, we of course chose the Unbeatable Squirrel Girl. We all pitched in on the costume and I think he pulled it off pretty well.

Kyle Gong

RYAN: I rate your manager: AWESOME. Also please tell me he came in with those plastic bags of nuts tied to his belt before the costume was ever conceived of, because that is a new level of efficient snacking.

**ERICA: YES YES YES

and versatility. Maybe like Kraven, my dogs need to find a new enemy.

I have attempted to read Squirrel Girl comics to my dogs in the hopes of changing their minds. Sadly, they are too distracted by the squirrels outside to ever sit still for enough time.

Max D.
Los Angeles, CA

RYAN: My first dog, Kita, hated squirrels too (or really just loved to bark at them and chase them off the deck? It is impossible to say). My current dog, Noam Chompsky, doesn't really notice squirrels, but I do, and if I'm behind on a deadline it's like they're all saying "hey stop hanging out with your dog in the park and go work, slacker." So I think it's fair to say that, like you, my relationship with squirrels has become... more complicated?

ERICA: As I've mentioned in the letters before, I was bitten by a squirrel (remember kids, they're wild animals!) and had to get tested for rabies. It took me a long time to come back around to squirrels but I was pretty okay with them again before I started on the book. Now my goal is to find someone who has a pet squirrel so that I can play with it.

Hi there!

I would like to start with thanking you guys for providing me with a comic that is most definitely worth spending my money on; I buy them both in digital and physical copies, because when living in Denmark it takes a while for the magazines to arrive and I'm not always a patient person - not when it comes to things like this ;)

Secondly, OH MY GOSH! I've never had that much attention on any of my cosplays, as when you retweeted and blogged my Star Trek/Squirrel Girl picture, as well as my "standard" ones (not that there's anything ordinary about Doreen.)

I fell in love with her after reading the first volume, with her positive attitude, her humor and her style, and knew right away that I had to make her my newest cosplay, and I love it! She has practical pockets (lots of room for nuts) and while my tail is a tiny bit heavy, it's also a build-in chair! And people loved it when I brought it to the latest con! I even made a nice bunch of her trading cards, just for props .I am introducing her to everyone I know, and the last time I saw my five year old sister, her very first thing to say was not "hi," but rather "you're a squirrel!" because she'd seen the pictures online.

I love Doreen, Tippy Toe and you guys, and I am happy to spread the word!

Peace out!
Stine Fuchs

Denmark

RYAN: Stine, your cosplay is, and I say this without hyperbole, OFF THE HOOK. Holy cow. Also, it's such a thrill to see cosplay for Squirrel Girl! Especially when it's so great. I love that you made more Deadpool cards too - they're so much fun to write (AS YOU HAVE NOW DISCOVERED) that I'm sure there'll be more here in the future! In conclusion, you are awesome (and thank you so much for buying every issue - TWICE!) and we are in your debt. Keep spreading the word!!

ERICA: Your Star Trek Squirrel Girl is amazing, as is your Squirrel Girl Squirrel Girl. For readers who haven't seen it, it's on our tumblr (see below).

The Deadpool cards are AMAZING. I love that you're drawing them yourself too. Keep sending us photos, okay? We will retweet ALL OF THEM.

RYAN: Finally, I'd like to dedicate this issue to Hester the sugar glider, pictured below. While not technically a squirrel (sugar gliders look similar to flying squirrels but had a different evolutionary path!), she was the pet of our editor Wil and his wife, Julia, and she had an awesome ten-year run. She was loved so much, and will be missed.

ERICA: She's beautiful. I'm sorry she's gone, Wil, but you've had a great many years with her and that's what's important.

Next: It's The End Of The Squirrel-D As We Know It!

On Sale Next Month!

Attention Squirrel Scouts! Make sure to check out our production blog, **unbeatablesquirrelgirl.tumblr.com**, where we post behind-the-scenes stuff on how the book gets made, along with all sorts of cool things *you* make: fan art, cosplay, whatever!

the unbeatable Squirrel Girl

Doreen Green isn't just a first-year computer science student: she secretly also has all the powers of both squirrel and girl. She uses her amazing abilities to fight crime **and** be as awesome as possible. You know her as...**The Unbeatable Squirrel Girl**. Let's catch up with what she's been up to until now, with...

Squirrel Girl *in a nutshell*

Nancy W. @sewwiththeflo
If I don't come back, I want my epitaph to read "HERE LIES NANCY WHITEHEAD: SHE WENT TO ASGARD AND DIED AND IT WAS TOTALLY WORTH IT."

Nancy W. @sewwiththeflo
Koi Boi and Chipmunk Hunk and @unbeatablesg all stayed behind, so I need y'all to make sure one of them takes care of this for me.

Squirrel Girl! @unbeatablesg
@sewwiththeflo dude, you're not going to DIE in ASGARD!! you got a current AND a former Thor watching your back! COME ON

Nancy W. @sewwiththeflo
@unbeatablesg It was a humblebrag, SG. A humbleepitaph.

Squirrel Girl! @unbeatablesg
@sewwiththeflo only you would brag by updating your followers on what your GRAVESTONE should read.

Nancy W. @sewwiththeflo
@unbeatablesg #personalbranding

Tony Stark @starkmantony
@unbeatablesg Hey, just looking at a report that says you're fighting "a giant monster god-squirrel from Asgard named 'Ratatoskr'"

Tony Stark @starkmantony
@unbeatablesg Can't help noticing that before I knew you, there were precisely zero evil squirrel-gods running around NYC.

Squirrel Girl! @unbeatablesg
@starkmantony uh that's funny because before I knew YOU there were precisely zero IRON MONGERS and MADAME MASQUES running around NYC!!

Squirrel Girl! @unbeatablesg
@starkmantony haha okay, so, i got those from a website that lists villains you've defeated? but they're like, bonkers

Squirrel Girl! @unbeatablesg
@starkmantony dude you fought a BIG WHEEL named "BIG WHEEL" that was invented by one "Jackson WHEELE"??? that's SINCERELY AMAZING.

Tony Stark @starkmantony
@unbeatablesg Can't talk, gotta get back to my very important world-class CEO work. Just take care of the squirrel thing.

Squirrel Girl! @unbeatablesg
@starkmantony obviously i'm gonna do that! quick question before I go though. just one super-quick question, okay?

Squirrel Girl! @unbeatablesg
@starkmantony when he said he was gonna take over earth, did you tell him he "spoke" too soon and is in "wheely" big trouble now or WHAT

Squirrel Girl! @unbeatablesg
So um, I kinda beat up the Avengers? In 26 seconds?? But they were being mind-controlled so it's okay

HULK @HULKYSMASHY
@unbeatablesg HULK WAS NOT PRESENT FOR THIS BUT HULK THINKS ABOUT BEATING UP AVENGERS ALL THE TIME

Squirrel Girl! @unbeatablesg
@HULKYSMASHY haha, well, they sassed my pals!! they were SO RUDE!

HULK @HULKYSMASHY
@unbeatablesg HULK WOULD LIKE TO BELIEVE THERE IS ALWAYS TIME FOR POLITENESS

Squirrel Girl! @unbeatablesg
@HULKYSMASHY dude! you are blowing my mind here!! i had no idea you thought this way!

Squirrel Girl! @unbeatablesg
@HULKYSMASHY hulk smash...my prejudices against giant green rage monsters!!

search!

- #asgard
- #catsgard
- #ratatoskrage
- #breakfastmeets
- #seeyouinoctober

CAT THOR
IN
~~NICE TO MEET YOU~~
NICE TO BEAT YOU
CAT THOR ONCE AGAIN BATTLES THE FROST GIANT SCHNAUZERS
GRRR!
LAUFUR, I DECLARE THEE AND THY ALLIES
TO BE BAD DOGS!!
SMAK SMAK SMAK
HAH HAH HAH
CATTHOR WINS AGAIN!
HEY!
AND NOW I MUST RETURN ONCE MORE TO CATSGARD!
FORSOOOOTH!!
CATSGARD
THERE HE MEETS WITH MEOWDIN, THE ALLPAWTHER!
DID YOU DEFEAT THE GIANTS, MY SON?
VERILY, FATHER, FOR THEE MIGHT SAY I GAVE THEM... CLAWS FOR CONCERN?
AY, THEE PROCLAIMS THAT EVERY TIME
NOW LET'S FLEX OUR MUSCLES, AS IS THE TRADITION OF OUR PEOPLE!
AGREED!
THE END
A NANCY WHITEHEAD PRODUCTION
WORDS BY NANCY WHITEHEAD
PICTURES BY NANCY WHITEHEAD
CAT THOR WILL RETURN...
NEXT TIME I'M BORED IN CLASS!

Oh--
Asgard.
Oh WOW.

I must say, thy seer Wikipedia seems to know an awful lot about some *very* embarrassing subject matter!

In case you're wondering, these meetings between Nancy, the Thors, and Loki are taking place around 7am, Asgardian Standard Time. That's right. They're the breakfast meets.

Theory: if instead of "Earth" we called our planet "Where The Party's At," maybe more aliens would be contacting us and inquiring vis-a-vis joining the Friggin' party??

I don't worry about when it's too soon to say *"I love you."* I worry about when it's too soon to say *"I really, really like you and I'm glad we're friends, do you want to come over and maybe we'll get a pizza?"*

Squirrel Girl's *also* got a liberal idea of personal property ownership, jerks!!

Not bad for lyrics improvised on the spot, right?? I also would've accepted *"Can she beat Spider-Man? Evidence shows she can."*

And I never even got to make a sword and shield out of webbing either, *or* a fully-functional car! ***What a waste.***

Brothers, am I right? Always teasing each other, always turning their heads into cat versions of the other brother's head. Classic!

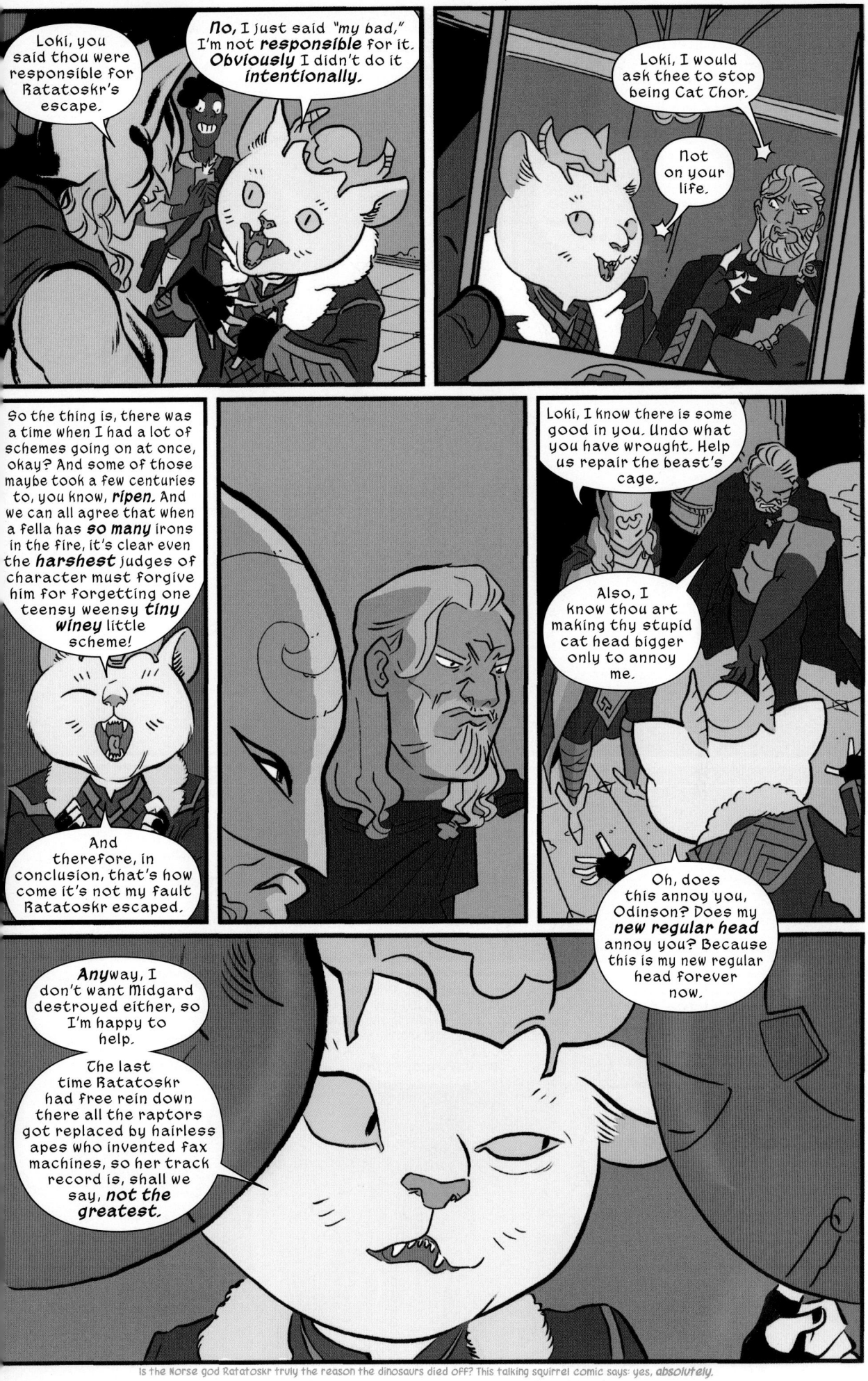

Is the Norse god Ratatoskr truly the reason the dinosaurs died off? This talking squirrel comic says: yes, *absolutely.*

People with bluetooth headsets: sorry for making them pop off your head in surprise right now, just as monocles did in times of yore.

Friends, I know right now you've paused reading while you frantically try to remember everything that could sound like "KASHOOOM"--
but I have some good news! The answer is on the very next page!

Hey. Ratatoskr!
Stop trying to make my friend go nuts.
Ahhhh, Nancy!! It's the perfect line!!

Too late, Asgardians. This world is already done for, and Squirrel Girl will soon help me destr--
Incoming!!

CHUUUUUUUUUUUUK!!*
*Translation: Here comes the Tippy-Toe Fuzzball Special, chumpo!!

SWOOSH

Missed me.
SMAK!

Yeah, wasn't aiming for you.

CHUKKA CHUK CHUK!*
CHITT CHITTY!**
You of all people should know a clever squirrel can hide something in her tail, Ratatoskr.
*These'll protect you from her, Doreen!
**Also, it was really frustrating that nobody could understand me in Asgard, but we'll talk about that later!!
Give me that!!
What's that, Ratatoskr? Can't quite hear you over my earplugs, jerk!!
ARRGH!
Stupid Thor!
KLANG
KLANG
Ow!
Ow!!
KLANG
Actually, that was me. Hey Ratatoskr. I'm cosplaying as "Cat Thor," and that hammer was... "Mewnir"?
Squirrel Girl! Asgard was awesome and I'll explain later!!
CATCH
This is the real Thor.
KLANGGGG
ARRRGHHH
RRRRGGGHHHH
FWOOOOSH

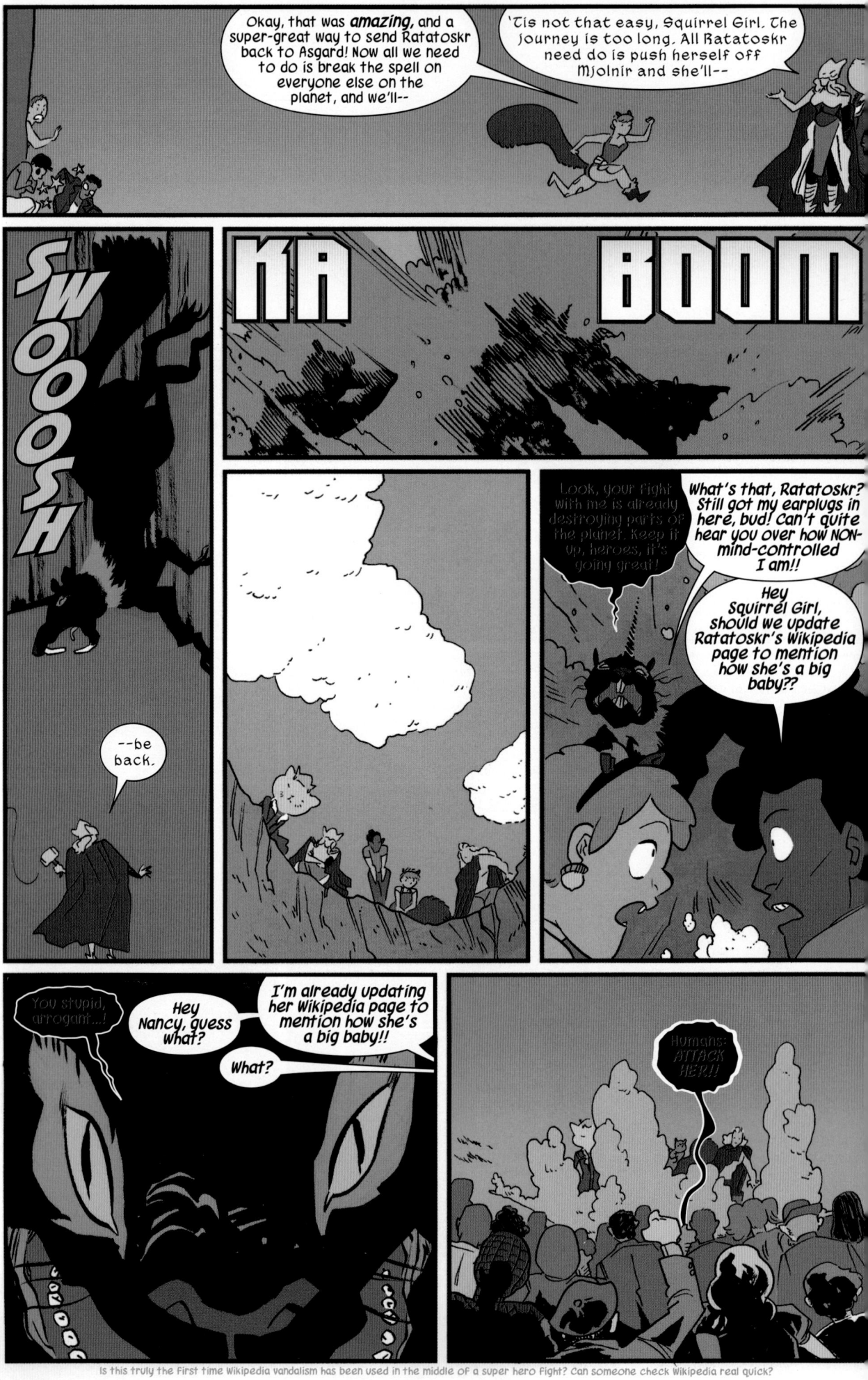

Is this truly the first time Wikipedia vandalism has been used in the middle of a super hero fight? Can someone check Wikipedia real quick?

Thou hast trash-talked the trash-talker.
Yeah man, if she's angry, she might get sloppy. But go, keep her busy! I got a plan, all I need is a megaphone!
Squirrel Girl, thou cannot take on this mob alone. Ratatoskr has several heroes in her thrall.
Go!! I got this!!

ROOF!
Hey. Any friend of Nancy's.
Awww!
Thanks, dude!!

Attention, crazy mind-controlled mob!!
I know how Ratatoskr works, how she preys on your insecurity and jealousy to make you attack others because you feel bad about yourself. But you don't have to let that happen!
The only reason you'd do that is if you're ***ashamed*** of your insecurities!

I am a super hero and I am here to tell you that feeling insecure is nothing to be ashamed of.
We all have anxieties, but--and this may sound crazy--they're actually kinda what make us awesome!
Real talk: I was insecure about my own fighting and jealous of other people's skills. So you know what I did?
I got better at fighting!!

Envy isn't about the person you're jealous of: it's about your***self.*** It's your mind telling you ***exactly*** what you want, and you know what that is? That's friggin' ***self-knowledge,*** and it's the most valuable thing in the universe.
It's how we tell ourselves what we need to work on in order to make ourselves the better, happier, more awesome versions of ***us*** that we deserve to be!

So what do you say, *huh?* Let's do it! Let's not let our feelings ***control*** us, but let's instead ***use*** those feelings, turning them towards productive personal growth instead of petty acts of violence!
Let's be the change we're insecure and jealous about in the world!!

Get her!! Tear her apart!
Aw frig, dang it!!

Aw, pals! And a happy ending for the two brothers! Now as long as you don't read *Loki: Agent of Asgard #10*, this happy feeling can last ***forever!!***

A Few Days Later...
You guys, I'm still choked Girl Squirrel was a fake!
Sorry I Got Mind-Controlled Again
I want there to be real super-powered pets. How great would that be?
Great for fish, clearly, but I wouldn't want to face down a bear with laser vision and a healing factor.
We could take 'em, Ken! We almost destroyed the world when we were mind-controlled!
CHITT
Oh. Sorry again about that, by the way.
You were mind-controlled dudes, dudes. Again: no apologies necessary!
Should we get back to it? I've only got a few more minutes before class.
Right. Tippy?
Chitt!
CHIT
Okay, this is basic, but that's "Chitt," with a long "tik" at the end. Two Ts. That's a vowel sound there, so getting it wrong is the difference between "I raised my hand to block the sun" and "I raised my hind to block the sun."
"Chiitt."
It's not that different than Chipmunkese, actually. "Chitt."
"Chuiiit."
Good! Better! Man, you guys better watch out. Keep up this level of progress, and--
--well...
...you'll be unbeatable.
The End!

Written by
Ryan North

Art by
Erica Henderson

Color Art by
Rico Renzi

Lettering and Production by
VC's Clayton Cowles

Cover Artist	Erica Henderson
Assistant Editor	Jon Moisan
Editor	Wil Moss
Executive Editor	Tom Brevoort
Editor in Chief	Axel Alonso
Chief Creative Officer	Joe Quesada
Publisher	Dan Buckley
Executive Producer	Alan Fine

Squirrel Girl will return...
...in our second #1 issue this year because SHE'S JUST THAT GOOD.

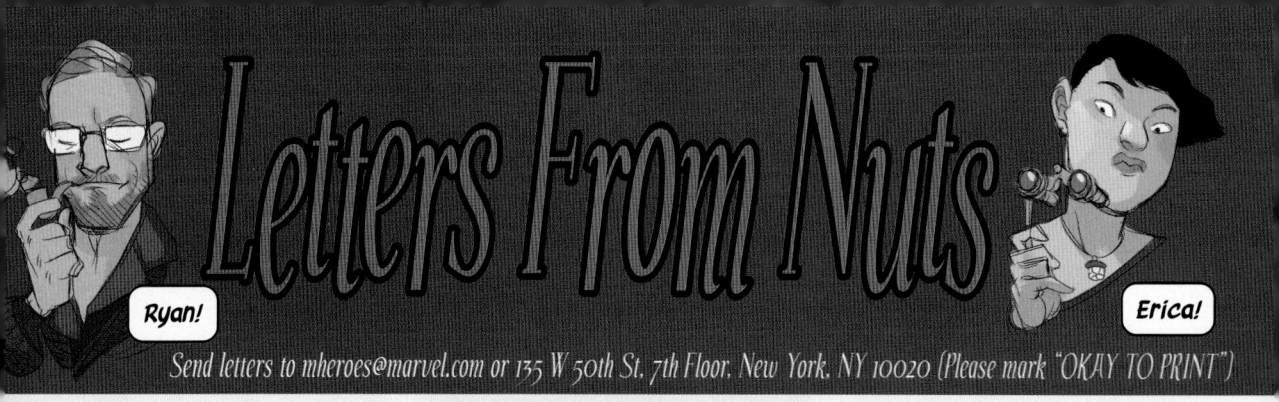

ear Ryan and Erica,

I am the paleontologist boyfriend that Amanda e squirrel biologist mentioned when she wrote to ou back in issue #5. I study predator-prey arms ces in tyrannosaurs and duckbills. Thanks for sponding to Amanda's letter. She is now totally sessed with your comic (which I also think is elightful). Although, I am worried that I should art being a little jealous of that Chipmunk Hunk llow. I notice that, unlike Doreen, he doesn't have utility belt. I assume this means that, much like real chipmunk, he carries all his hero gear in his eek pouches, which is gross. Yeah, Chipmunk unk is gross. Why don't you go ahead and make at canon? Also, is it possible to get any of that weet "Eat Nuts and Kick Butts" merchandise?

Anyway, I am glad to see you haven't taken manda up on her suggestion to introduce a aleontological comic foil who is dreadfully boring comparison with Squirrel Girl and her other iends. But I do have an alternative suggestion r you. Amanda never told you about her squirrel search. She studies how the personalities of tle squirrels relate to their siblings and how their ersonalities change as the squirrels mature. She oes that by catching squirrels (which are complete uckers for peanut butter) and recording their ehaviors when placed in a white-walled glass-oofed contraption filled with fake tunnel entrances nd mirrors. It's all totally humane, but doesn't at sound like a premise for one of those alien-sychological-observer or hypno/illusionist super llains? Chew it over, and thanks again.

W. Scott Persons, IV

P.S. Erica, thanks for giving your tyrannosaur ome protofeathers and for getting your pterosaur's ing membrane attachments right back in issue 5. Yours are much better than in that recently equeled popular dinosaur movie franchise (the ame escapes me, but you know the one I mean).

P.P.S. Attached is a photo of me visiting with one f Amanda's research subjects and also a photo of manda and me together, so you'll know that I am ho I say I am and not just some nut . . . errr you et the point.

RYAN: Okay this is the best letter ever, and everyone else is now on notice: your letters have to be at LEAST as awesome as this, so please feature a) squirrels b) love and c) interesting squirrel facts in all future letters. I personally just started reading a book about squirrel facts, and did you know there are squirrels on five different continents? They're so widespread that THE SUN NEVER SETS ON SQUIRRELS. There is no way this fact is not making it into a future comic, so uh, when you read it later on try to act surprised.

ERICA: TAKE THAT, HOLLYWOOD. SOME PEOPLE care about being up to date on the latest scientific knowledge on dinosaurs. Listen, we all like Charles Knight, but the golden age of paleontology is over, guys.

P.S. I hope you guys keep writing in.

P.P.S. Now that I know their weakness I'm going to lure in ALL THE SQUIRRELS.

P.P.S. Oh god, are we those people that nobody wants to see movies with because we're going to go on about how Ron Silver being defeated at the end of *Time Cop* makes no scientific sense?

P.P.P.S. Don't watch *Time Cop*.

Dear lovely Erica and Ryan,

Thank you, thank you, thank you for UNBEATABLE SQUIRREL GIRL! With your super-powers combined, you have brought Doreen Green to life in the absolute best way! I love your comic so much, I threw a Marvel themed party for my 30th birthday JUST so I could be Squirrel Girl. And the best part? My best friend Jack surprised me with a squirrel battle against one of Doreen's greatest adversaries...Doctor Doom! Take a look for yourself! #SquirrelSelfie! Thanks Erica and Ryan for doing what you do! Long live Squirrel Girl!

Brittany

R: This is amazing, and I've got to go to way better parties! Great costumes too. I notice Doom's covered in squirrels: confound those wretched rodents!!

E: HM. Next year is my 30th. I may need to steal some ideas from you. PLUS my boyfriend LOVES Doom and does have a couple of teeny scars on his face to make the whole thing even more accurate. HMMMMMMMMMMMMM.

Dear Erica and Ryan,

My dad and I have been reading this awesome comic, and I love it! For this year's Comic-Con in San Diego I tried to get my sister to come dressed as Tippy Toe, but she wouldn't! I have a question though, if Squirrel Girl was in a big crowd of people in her costume, wouldn't her tail keep hitting people in the face? Or would she have to flatten her tail across her back?

Your Inquisitive Fan,
Neva Devine, Age 12

R: I have paid a lot of attention to our cosplaying fans (on account of how they are the best) and most attach the tail via a concealed hook at the back of the vest, which means the tail always stays in place. It shouldn't be hitting people in the face that way, but will still look great! We've reblogged a couple of tutorials, which you can find on the cosplay tag of our unbeatablesquirrelgirl.tumblr.com site!

Anyway, to answer your actual question, yes absolutely Squirrel Girl would hit people in the face with her tail, but only those that deserved it.

E: In a crowd situation I think it would be easier to wrap the tail around herself like in the laser defense system scene in issue #2.

Dear USG team, makers of sheer delight,

I don't have an adorable baby squirrel to send you a photo of, but I do have the second printing of USG #4, which is almost as good, and coincidentally has become my all-time favorite comic issue ever. Of all the times. How will I ever beat that? It's impossible! I really liked how you had Doreen handle Galactus--getting him take-out--Beautiful. I love you crazy nuts for doing this comic. It's uproarious, and I keep getting people to read it. I just finished reading #6, and I can't wait for the next issue. If Squirrel Girl and Magneto form a road-trip duo, I think I'll pop from sheer giggles. Everything about this comic is delightful, and in the midst of the super-serious SECRET WARS and Mister Fantastic's moody melodrama, sheer delight is such a great change of tone. It's immensely needed, and positively needed.

John Polkowske

R: Aw thanks! That's super sweet. I like the idea of Squirrel Girl and Magneto going on a road-trip and the car runs out of gas and Doreen makes Magneto "push" the car with his powers the rest of the way. That's my pitch: a put-upon Magneto and carefree Squirrel Girl discover America, and also...friendship. Marvel, you read your own letters pages, right?? [Ed. note: Only the ones that bag on *Time Cop*.]

E: Hey, he should push the car the whole way. We're not in a place where we should be wasting fuel when we don't have to! Plus, that way, they can tool around in a really sweet vintage ride without worrying about it breaking down all the time.

Hey Squirrel Girl team,

A lot of my friends who are ladies often talk

about their crushes on fictional characters, and it has been something I respected but never really "got." But now that I may or may not have a crush on Squirrel Girl, it's possible that I maaaay see their points. I mean, it is likely that Doreen is super passionate about her interests and would probably have great conversations about squirrels, computer science and squirrel computer science on dates. Plus there is a possibility that she's a super caring, sweet person that would make anyone super happy. It also may be true that she's super cute and strong and awkward in an adorable way? But none of this is, of course, confirmed. Just like my crush on Squirrel Girl. Which is totally up for debate and not confirmed in any way.

(Possibly?) JD Boucher

R: I have a big crush on Commander Data from *Star Trek,* so I understand you. It's more of a friendship crush though. I just want to hang out with robots and the robot-adjacent!

E: I'm pretty sure my first crush ever was on Race Bannon. I totally get it.

Hi Ryan! Hi Erica!

SQUIRREL GIRL is a grand book, yielding laughs and thoughts and an appreciation of pictures. I like it and buy it often.

But I'm afraid there's a bug in your sixth comic. In the front menu, I (naturally) picked Dazzler and Devil Dinosaur as the newest friends of the unbeatable Squirrel Girl, but the "Answer Inside" gave Chipmunk Hunk and Koi Boi. It's 100% reproducible. It even lets me select zero characters but then presents these two.

In case anyone else is facing this issue, I've attached a fix:

Up with squirrels!
Cheston

R: Cheston, I love this. Also: Thank you for the bug report; it has been confirmed on our end and will hopefully be corrected in a future team-up.

E: Marvel IS restarting WHAT IF? Man, I also hope that Marvel reads its own letter columns. [Ed. note: Only the ones with embarrassing *Star Trek* crush revelations.]

Good day, fine folks at Squirrel Girl's headquarters!

This comic brings me more joy than I know what to do with! It's the funniest comic and my absolute favorite. Doreen is my kind of hero--she's so positive, tough, way cool and a total sweetheart. The artwork is endearing, the writing is hilarious, and the animal rhyming names are the best. Thank you so much for this book. You guys are super awesome. My life is better for having read it.

Will you be restarting the series this fall after SECRET WARS ends?? I just looked through the All-New All-Different Marvel Previews and it wasn't in there. I'm worried, to say the least. Are you planning for Superior Squirrel Girl? All-New Squirrel Girl? Old Gal Doreen? Squirrel-Verse event? Squirrel Wars?? I'll take any Doreen Green you wanna serve up.

I've never written in to a comic before, but this book is so great that getting my picture in an issue of SQUIRREL GIRL is now on my bucket list. Here I am reading my books in a tree, so as to be closer to Tippy Toe and Doreen:

Making Mine Marvel, and wishing you all the nuts,
Molly J. Santa Maria
San Diego, CA

R: This is ALSO amazing. Thank you, Molly! And I have good news: we ARE continuing after SECRET WARS! We're taking a (short!) break, but then we'll be restarting with a new #1 in October. Same characters! Same creative team! Just a new story that builds on everything here. Also, while it's not "Old Man Doreen," you'll be able to get even more Squirrel Girl then, as she'll be in the NEW AVENGERS book too!

E: "Old Man Doreen" is another one for WHAT IF. Also, consider that photo PRINTED.

Erica and Ryan,

Forget all other work commitments, social obligations and personal hobbies, okay? I'm going to need this series to go on FOREVER. Will you accept haikus as a form of reimbursement? Here's a small down payment:

Chik chukka chut chut
Chit chit chukka chitty chut
Chut chitty chukka

Brittany Meredith

R: Ran that by Tippy and she said it was FLATTERING and SAUCY, so thank you!

E: WHAT MAKES YOU THINK WE MIGHT WANT TO STOP?

Erica, Ryan, and Rico,

Hi! I love SQUIRREL GIRL, I've been reading since issue #1, and the story has gotten better and better with each book -- which seems impossible because it's already so amazing. I loved the inclusion of the Avengers in #7. Black Widow and Squirrel Girl in the same panel was like a most wonderful dream... That quickly came to end end because... well...insert spoiler here.I'm really looking forward to the next issue, especially because Ratatoskr is an extremely-scary-looking squirrel with unicorn qualities. An evil unicorn. And I didn't know those types existed.

So yeah, you're all amazing and I love your book and Doreen and Tippy-Toe. Thanks for a great comic book! (:

Brake for squirrels!
Erin

PS: Way back in February when someone at the comic book store told me the person who did the coloring for SQUIRREL GIRL worked at the store, I was blown away and totally geeked out. Thanks Rico!

E: Haha. I liked Black Widow better in #5 because she wasn't mind-controlled into being a jerk. She's so much fun either way though. Ratatoskr is great. I haven't had a chance to draw monsters for a while so it's been a treat!

Friends,

I'm a teacher in North Carolina and picked up the first issues of UNBEATABLE SQUIRREL GIRL for our after school comic club. After reading the first two comics, SQUIRREL GIRL became a pa of my personal pull-list, as well as a title the kid couldn't wait for more of. Thanks for such a fur positive book!

Additionally, around issue #4 our daughte Penelope was born. I'm pretty sure she's a hug fan because between naps she has been fightin crime under the guise of "Sugar Glider":

Does Squirrel Girl need a sidekick? Keep up th great work.

Joel Richardsor
Washington, N

R: Can we just turn this letters page into a "adorable pictures of fans" page instead? I an so into this. Welcome to the world, Penelope! had to wait until I was actually writing a book t be published in a letters page; you've got a hug head start (and awesome costume!).

E: Did you make that or is there a store tha sells tiny super hero apparel for babies? Is it i North Carolina? I'm amazed it took this long t break into this untapped market!

Hi Erica and Ryan,

I've been picking up UNBEATABLE SQUIRRE GIRL since the beginning, and it's just terrifi (although it takes twice as long to read because c the tiny type at the bottom of the pages). That saic why I'm writing is to thank you on behalf of m five-year-old daughter, Thessaly. She loves comics and we always read SQUIRREL GIRL together s she can find out what's happening with Tippy-Toe.

A while ago, we played through *Lego Marve Heroes* together, and after beating the end boss Galactus, she developed a persistent fear that h was coming to eat her. That same week, SQUIRRE GIRL #4 came out, and as soon as I got home, handed it to her to read. No more Galactus fear --she even wrote him a note telling him she love him! Thanks a lot, guys (not only for helping ou my girl, but for advancing a plausible theory of jus why Galactus can never manage to devour Earth)- you've earned these two readers.

Bob Britten (and Thessaly

R: Terrific! And tell Thessaly that when I wrot the story it was after playing that very sam game! I took a photo of Galactus and Squirre Girl together (you can unlock her, she's by th dockyard!) and sent it to my wife with the subjec line "story idea."

E: Oh my god, everything about that story i great and I can't even.

New Series. New Avenger (!). Still Eats Nuts and Kicks Butts!

See you in October!
(And keep the letters coming in the meantime!)
- Ryan, Erica, Rico, Clayton, Jon and Wil!

Attention, Squirrel Scouts! Make sure to check out our production blog, **unbeatablesquirrelgirl.tumblr.com**, where we post behind-the-scenes stuff on how the book gets made, along with all sorts of cool things *you* make: fanart, cosplay, whatever!

Hi Ratatoskr,

Okay, so you're probably wondering what just happened. I'm sorry, I KNOW our plan was always for you to get loose and have free rein over Midgard, distracting everyone in Asgard long enough for ME to take over here. Change of plan, buddy.

Turns out this was just a test, a trial run. And yeah, you're back in jail, but now we know EXACTLY what the heroes will do to stop us. We know their moves, their weaknesses, and when I bust you out next time, we won't be destroying the Earth--we'll be destroying ASGARD HERSELF.

p.s.: okay, no, just kidding. I know that letter was what you were EXPECTING to read, but honestly I'm trying to be a better person, and part of that means not associating with the kind of people who pull me back into my old habits. I saved one of the Ten Realms today, Ratatoskr. I mean, I saved it from OUR plan...but still. You know what the best part of dressing up like Cat Thor is?

You actually feel like Cat Thor.

I think I'm gonna chase that feeling for a while.

p.p.s.: I enclosed a present. I know you two don't get along but I figured you might like some company.

p.p.p.s.: If you pull the string, she talks!

YOU'VE SEEN MY FRIEND DOREEN EAT NUTS AND KICK BUTTS IN THE MARVEL *NOW!*
NOW, REVISIT THE MARVEL *THEN!* FOR SOME EXTRA-SPECIAL BONUS TAILS!

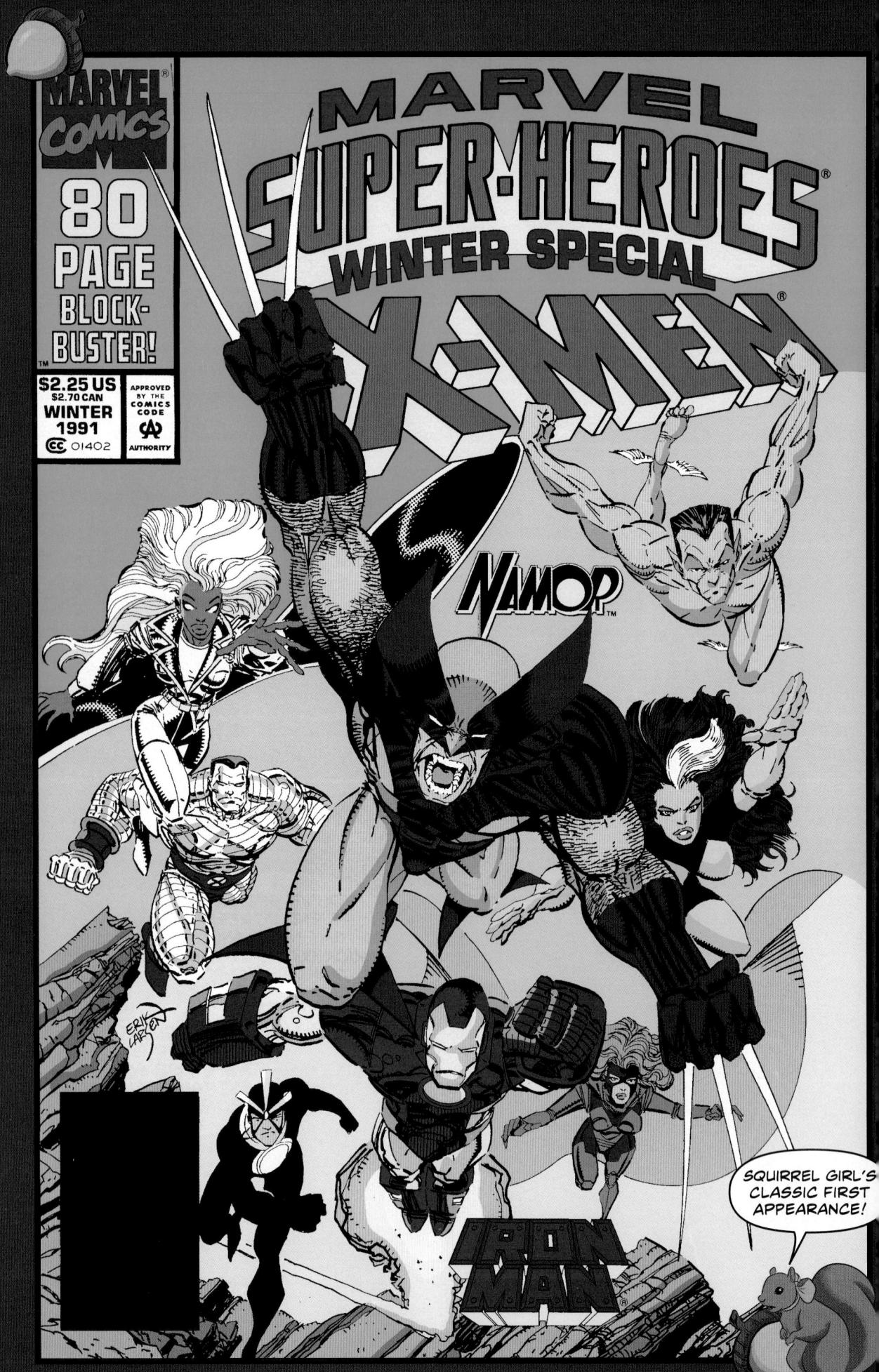

MARVEL SUPER-HEROES #8

STAN LEE PRESENTS:
the coming of... SQUIRREL GIRL!
ONE GOOD THING ABOUT BEING ENCASED IN A HEAD-TO-TOE SUIT OF CYBERNETIC BODY ARMOR...
IRON MAN
SO FAR, SO GOOD.
PING
MY EXPERIMENTAL ON-BOARD COLLISION AVOIDANCE RADAR IS WORKING PERFECTLY-- AUTOMATICALLY VECTORING ME AWAY FROM OBJECTS IN MY FLIGHT PATH.
NO ONE CAN SEE YOU SWEAT.
STEVE DITKO - PLOT, PENCILS, INKS
WILL MURRAY - SCRIPT
CHRISTIE SCHEELE - COLORS
BRAD K. JOYCE - LETTERER

TONY STARK IS SWEATING NOW.
PING!

WITH GOOD REASON.
PING!

PING!
HE CAN'T SEE A THING...EXCEPT INTERNAL DIGITAL READOUTS.

AND HE'S ZIG-ZAGGING THROUGH A CHOKED STAND OF TREES NEAR STARK ENTERPRISES AT OVER 90 MILES AN HOUR!
PING!
NOW I KNOW HOW THE EARLY ASTRONAUTS FELT--BLASTING THROUGH SPACE STRAPPED INTO A WINDOWLESS CAPSULE.

BOOT JETS LIFTING ME UP...
MUST BE A HORIZONTAL BARRIER DIRECTLY AHEAD.
PING!
PING!

OKAY, TONY. I GUESS YOU'VE GOT A BACK-UP IN THE ALWAYS-POSSIBLE EVENT YOU'RE BLINDED OR BLACK OUT IN FLIGHT.
PROVIDED YOU SURVIVE THE TEST RUN.
UNBEKNOWNST TO THE ARMORED AVENGER, A TWITCHING-TAILED FIGURE CROUCHES ON A TREE-BRANCH, WAITING TO POUNCE.

WHICH IT DOES WITH UNERRING SKILL.
WHA...?! EITHER I'VE BEEN ATTACKED...
...OR THE CAR SYSTEM HAS JUST DEVELOPED A MAJOR BUG.
WHOEVER YOU ARE, YOU'VE MADE A BIG MISTAKE.
JUST BECAUSE I'M WEARING THIS ALLOY BLINDER DOESN'T MEAN I CAN'T DEAL WITH YOU!
CAN'T SHAKE HIM.
AND HIS PROXIMITY IS CONFUSING THE CAR SYSTEM.
ALL RIGHT, LET'S SEE EXACTLY WHO YOU ARE!
NOT YET! NOT YET!
SOMETHING WHIPPED INTO MY EYES. FEELS LIKE...
FUR?
BEEP
BEEP BEEP
UH-OH! CAR OVERLOAD WARNING SENSOR JUST KICKED IN!
FLAMEOUT!
VOOF!
VOOF!
BOOT-JETS COULDN'T TAKE THE STRAIN!

ONE COLD COMFORT.
HE'S GOING DOWN WITH ME.

WHAT ON EARTH?

HI! I'M SQUIRREL GIRL.
SQUIRREL GIRL?

YEAH, NEAT NAME, HUH?

WELL, IT DOES RHYME.
WHAT'S THE IDEA OF JUMPING ME?

I JUST WANTED TO SHOW YOU HOW ROUGH AND TOUGH I CAN REALLY BE.
ROUGH AND TOUGH?

I FIGURED I'D HAVE TO PROVE MYSELF BEFORE YOU'D TAKE ME ON AS YOUR FIGHTING PARD.
PARD?

WHAT MAKES YOU THINK I WANT OR NEED A PARTNER?
EVERY HERO SHOULD HAVE A PARTNER. DON'T YOU KNOW THAT?

BESIDES, I LIKE YOU. YOU'RE MY FAVORITE AVENGER.

ALSO, I LIVE AROUND HERE, WHICH MEANS I CAN BE HOME IN TIME FOR DINNER.
UNLESS WE HAVE ANY REALLY BIG ADVENTURES IN CHINA OR MEXICO OR CONNECTICUT-- NEAT FARAWAY PLACES LIKE THAT.

I SEE, HOW OLD ARE YOU?
FIFTEEN--WELL, FIFTEEN NEXT JULY, ACTUALLY.
BUT WHO CARES ABOUT DUMB STUFF LIKE THAT?

DON'T YOU WANT TO SEE MY POWERS?
POWERS?

SURE. I HAVE PLENTY OF POWERS. I'M A MUTANT.
BUT DON'T TELL ANYONE, OKAY? IT'S KINDA EMBARRASSING.
MY LIPS ARE SEALED.
WHO WOULD BELIEVE ME?

WATCH THIS!

I CAN DO ANYTHING A REAL SQUIRREL CAN DO...

JUMP. CLIMB. HOP.
PLUS, I'M EXTRA, EXTRA NIMBLE.
AMAZING...

TA-DAH!
OKAY, YOU CAN HOP. SO CAN THE HULK.
WHAT ELSE?
WATCH. NOTHING UP MY SLEEVE.
PRESTO!
CHIK!
IT'S MY KNUCKLE SPIKE.
IRON MAN + SQUIRREL GIRL
I HAVE FINGER CLAWS, TOO, BUT THEY'RE TOO LITTLE FOR FIGHTING. GREAT FOR CLIMBING, THOUGH.
NOT EXACTLY IN WOLVERINE'S CLASS, ARE YOU?
YOU COULDN'T SHAKE ME OFF YOUR BACK SO EASY, COULD YOU?
GOOD POINT.
IS THAT ALL?
PLAYING HARD TO GET, HUH?
CHECK IT OUT. I CAN CHEW THROUGH SOLID WOOD WITH THIS BABY. GROSS, HUH?
IS THAT... TAIL REAL?
MY MOM THINKS IT'S THE CUTEST THING. BUT SHE DOESN'T HAVE TO HIDE IT IN HER JEANS.
SO WHAT'S THE VERDICT, AVENGER?
I CAN CALL YOU THAT, CAN'T I?
SQUIRRELS... THEY'RE RODENTS, AREN'T THEY?
WELL, YEAH. SORT OF. BUT THEY'RE NOT RATS OR ANYTHING.
WE'RE MUCH PRETTIER.
WE?
I CAN TELL YOU'RE NOT IMPRESSED.
OH! I FORGOT TO MENTION--I CAN TALK LIKE A SQUIRREL, TOO!

LISTEN.
CHITTY CHIK CHUK!
UH, VERY NICE. REALLY. YOU CAN STOP NOW.
CUK CUK CUK
DIDN'T I SOUND JUST LIKE A SQUIRREL?
YOU'VE CONVINCED ME. BUT I WOULDN'T EXACTLY CALL THAT A POWER.
ACTUALLY, THERE'S MORE TO IT THAN THAT...
WONDERFUL. MY WOULD-BE PARTNER, WHO TALKS LIKE A SQUIRREL.
CUK CUK CUK CUK CUK CUK CUK
WHAT?
ABOUT TIME YOU GUYS SHOWED UP.
THESE ARE YOURS?
THEY UNDERSTAND EVERYTHING I SAY!
CUK CHRT
CUK CUK CUK
HOW DO YOU GET THEM OFF?
EASY. YOU JUST GO 'CHUTTY CHET CHET!'
OF COURSE.
CHITTY
CUK CHRRT?

YOU KNOW, I'LL BET THE X-MEN WOULD BE VERY, VERY INTERESTED IN TALKING TO YOU.
NO WAY!
SPANK
GUK

I DON'T WANT ANYBODY TO KNOW I'M A MUTANT.
BESIDES, THEY'RE ALL SO STUCK UP--ESPECIALLY THAT OBNOXIOUS KITTY PRIDE.

I KNOW--WHY DON'T I INTRODUCE YOU TO CAPTAIN AMERICA? HE'S USUALLY OPEN TO NEW PARTNERS.
GUK
GUK
DOWN, MONKEY JOE!

I DON'T BELIEVE THIS. YOU'RE REJECTING ME!
IT'S NOTHING PERSONAL. HONESTLY.

I REALLY DON'T NEED A PARTNER. IRON MAN IS A SOLO ACT.
BUT...BUT YOU'RE MY PERSONAL HERO! YOU CAN'T SAY NO!

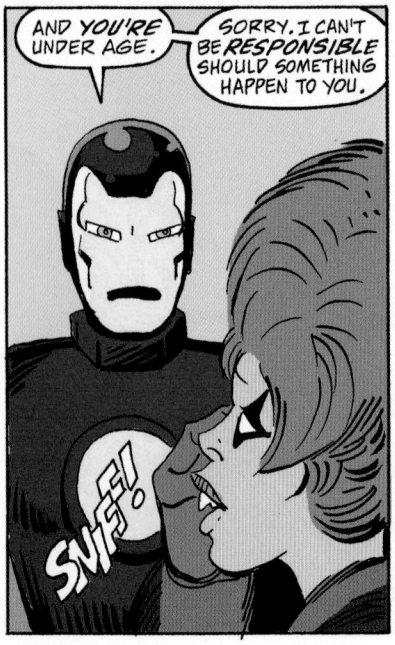
AND YOU'RE UNDER AGE.
SORRY. I CAN'T BE RESPONSIBLE SHOULD SOMETHING HAPPEN TO YOU.
SNIFF!

NOW IF YOU'LL EXCUSE ME, I'M RUNNING LATE.

WAIT! THERE'S ONE OTHER THING.

I DON'T KNOW HOW TO TELL YOU THIS, BUT ON MY WAY TO STARK ENTERPRISES, I-I KINDA SORTA HAD MY FIRST SUPERFIGHT.
CONGRATULATION CONGRATULATIONS.
WITH WHO?
I THINK.

WE WERE NEVER PROPERLY INTRODUCED, BUT HE WAS ONE OF THOSE ARMORED GUYS.
THE CRIMSON DYNAMO?

DON'T THINK SO. HE WAS GREEN.
NOT TITANIUM MAN? HE WEARS GREEN ARMOR. OR DID.

NO, THIS GUY'S ARMOR WAS GRAY. IT WAS HIS CLOTHES THAT WERE GREEN.
GRAY ARMOR... GREEN CLOTHES.

NOT--
PRECISELY, AVENGER.
DOCTOR DOOM.

HOLD STILL, PLEASE.
UGH!
CRUNN

OH NO! YOU HURT HIM!
HIS ELECTRONICS HAVE MERELY EXPERIENCED A PULSE-INDUCED INTERRUPTION.
AS FOR YOU, FOOLISH GIRL...
SSSSSSSSSS

BEHOLD, THE DOOMSHIP. AN INFILTRATION CRAFT SO LIGHTWEIGHT, SO DELICATELY BALANCED, IF NEED BE IT CAN CROSS A CONTINENT ON THE POWER OF A COMMON CAR BATTERY.
HUUU

ARE YOU ALL RIGHT? I'M REAL, REAL SORRY I GOT YOU INTO THIS.
IT ALL COMES BACK TO ME NOW...
WHAT?
NEVER MIND.
SOME KIND OF MANACLE... SURROUNDED BY AN ENERGY FIELD.
STAND BACK. I'M GOING TO... UGH... SHATTER THESE...BONDS.
PIECES MAY... UUHHH... FLY.
NO GO. THE HARDER I TRY, THE BRIGHTER THEY GLOW. SOME KIND OF ENERGY SINK, ACCORDING TO MY ONBOARD POWER INDICATORS.
THEY'RE DRAINING... MY ARMOR. CAN'T... BREAK THEM.
BUT YOU CAN'T FAIL! YOU'RE MY HERO!
THERE'S ALWAYS A FIRST TIME.
DO YOU HAVE ANY TOOLS IN THOSE POUCHES?
NO. THIS IS MY NUT STASH. I EAT THEM FOR ENERGY.
TRY SOME MACADAMIAS. THEY'RE GREAT FOR EXTRA PEP.

SOMEHOW, I DON'T THINK THEY'LL REPOWER MY ARMOR.
I ALSO HAVE PEANUTS, CASHEWS, ALMONDS, AND ACORNS.
THOSE I FEED TO MY CRITTERS.
NEVER MIND. ARE WE MOVING?

BRILLIANT OBSERVATION, AVENGER. WE ARE MOVING.
WE ARE ALSO NEARING THE ATLANTIC OCEAN, WHERE I INTEND TO DISPOSE OF YOUR BODIES.
BUT WE'RE NOT DEAD.

THANK YOU FOR REMINDING ME.
KLICK!

RRUM-RRUM
YII! WHERE'D THEY COME FROM?
IT'S NOT WHERE THEY CAME FROM THAT WORRIES ME. IT'S WHERE THEY'RE GOING.

RRUM-RRUM
AND THOSE WELLS IN THE OPPOSITE WALL ARE A MAJOR CLUE.

IRONIC, IS IT NOT, IRON MAN? YOU ARE ABOUT TO DIE BECAUSE THIS SLIP OF A FREAK EMBROILED YOU IN A QUARREL THAT WAS NOT YOURS.

VON DOOM, I DON'T SUPPOSE YOU'D CONSIDER LETTING HER GO?

ARE YOU MAD? TO WITNESS YOUR DESTRUCTION IS FITTING PUNISHMENT FOR HER MEDDLING IN MY AFFAIRS.
IGNORANCE OF THE NAME OF VICTOR VON DOOM ALONE IS SUFFICIENT INJURY TO MY VANITY TO SEAL HER FATE.
BIG TALK, VIC. BUT I GOTTA WARN YOU. I HAVE FRIENDS.

AH, YES. YOUR PRECIOUS SQUIRRELS. I AM SURE THEY WILL GET OVER YOUR LOSS SOON ENOUGH.
SQUIRRELS ARE EMOTIONALLY RESILIENT.

AND NOW, FAREWELL TO YOU BOTH.
RUDE DUDE, HUH?
AT LEAST WE'LL GO QUICK.

RRUM-RRUM-RRUM
IT WOULD BE QUICK IF THE SPIKES WERE POINTED. DOOM BLUNTED THEM, SO WE'LL BE CRUSHED TO DEATH SLOWLY.

UKK. DID I SAY I WAS SORRY?
SKIP THE APOLOGIES.
RRUM-RRUM-RRUM

IT'S UP TO YOU. I CAN'T BUDGE WITH MY SUIT DRAINED.
ME?

WHAT CAN I DO? I'M ONLY A...MISERABLE LITTLE RODENT.
JUST LIKE THE KIDS AT SCHOOL SAY.

RRUM-RRUM
TRY.
RRUM RRU
OKAY, OKAY. MAYBE THERE'S A SECRET WAY OUT OR SOMETHING.
LIKE IN A NANCY DREW.

I FOUND SOMETHING! BOY, THIS SUPERHEROING IS EASY.

DARN. IT'S ONLY A VENT.
WE'RE NOT VERY HIGH UP. I SEE TREES UNDER US.

RRUM
DOOM PROBABLY DOESN'T WANT TO SHOW UP ON RADAR.
THE SNEAK.
RRUM RRUM

MAYBE I CAN CALL FOR HELP.
CLIK CLIK CLIK

OR AT LEAST SAY GOODBYE TO MY SQUIRREL FRIENDS...
CHIT CHIT CHIT CHEET

ODD. THE STARBOARD PROXIMITY SCANNER IS FLASHING.
PIP PIP PIP

APPROACHING AIRCRAFT? AT THIS PALTRY ALTITUDE IMPOSSIBLE?

NOW THE PORT SCANNER HAS ACTIVATED, AS WELL.
AND VENTRAL.
PIP PIP
PIP PIP

WHATEVER PHENOMENON IS CAUSING THIS, IT RAPIDLY SURROUNDS MY DOOMSHIP.
THE VIEWER SHOULD REVEAL THE THREAT'S TRUE NATURE.

ARE THOSE... SQUIRRELS?
PIP PIP
PIP PIP PIP

THOSE CONFOUNDED RODENTS LEAPING ONTO OVER THE DOOM-SHIP.
PIP PIP

AND I AM UNABLE TO RECALIBRATE THE HYPER-SENSITIVE GRAVITY REPELLERS RAPIDLY ENOUGH TO COMPENSATE FOR THEIR CONSTANTLY SHIFTING WEIGHT.

NO MATTER, ONCE I AM OVER WATER, I WILL DROWN THE INFERNAL CREATURES.
POP
PIP PIP

CHUT?

FORGET YOUR PETS. CALL FOR HELP. HUMAN HELP.
THEY HAVE TO KNOW! WHO'S GOING TO FEED THEM IF I DIE!
WAIT! I SEE SOMETHING!
RRUMRUMRRUM

MONKEY JOE!
CHRTT?
CHRRT!

YOU CAN STOP STRUGGLING NOW. EVERYTHING'S GOING TO BE OKAY.
ARE YOU SERIOUS? WE'RE SECONDS AWAY FROM BEING CRUSHED TO DEATH.
RRUM RRUM RRUM

MONKEY JOE SAYS EVERYTHING WILL BE ALL RIGHT SOON.
IF YOU DON'T MIND, I'D JUST AS SOON GO DOWN FIGHTING.
OKAY. BUT SQUIRRELS DON'T LIE.
CHUT CHUT

I'LL TRY TO REMEMBER THAT.
HMMM. THERE GO THE LIGHTS.
TOLD YOU SO.

TRY TO BREAK FREE NOW.
MIGHT AS WELL... THESE MANACLES ARE DIMMING.

WHATEVER AGENCY IS AFFECTING THE SHIP, MY ARMOR SHOWS NO INTERNAL FLUCTUATIONS.
THERE!
CRACK!
CRACK!
IN FACT, I'M BACK TO FULL STRENGTH!
BRAAACK!
NOW FOR DOOM!
CUK
CUK
NOT AGAIN!
IT'S OKAY. THEY'RE ON OUR SIDE!
CHUT CHUT CHUT CHUT
I JUST TOLD THEM YOU'RE FRIENDLY.
CHIRRT
CHIRRT
CHIRRT
CHIRRT
TOO FRIENDLY.

NO WONDER THE POWER DIED. THIS WIRING HAS BEEN STRIPPED.
YOU KNOW HOW SQUIRRELS SOMETIMES GET INTO YOUR ATTIC AND CHEW THROUGH THE WIRING? TA-DAH!
I TAKE BACK EVERY BAD THING I EVER SAID ABOUT SQUIRRELS.
HEY! WHAT DID YOU SAY ABOUT SQUIRRELS THAT WAS BAD?
NEVER MIND. WE'D BETTER SEE ABOUT DOOM.
OH, DON'T WORRY ABOUT MR. GRIM MASK.
MY CRITTERS ARE TEACHING HIM A BIG LESSON.
CONFOUND THESE WRETCHED RODENTS!
FOR EVERY ONE I FLING AWAY, A DOZEN MORE VEX ME!
CLIK
CLIK
CLIK

INTOLERABLE! MY MUCH-VAUNTED TECHNOLOGY-- DECIMATED BY THESE GNAWING RODENTS!
CLIK!
CLIK!
CLIK!
CLIK!
CLIK!

TIME TO SURRENDER, VON DOOM. YOU'RE ARMOR LOOKS THOROUGHLY DISABLED TO ME.
NEVER!
CLIK!
CLIK!
CLIK!
BETTER THINK TWICE. I WON'T CALL THEM OFF UNTIL YOU DO!

DOOM WILL NEVER BE DEFEATED! NOT LIKE THIS!
CLIK
SIC 'IM, GUYS!

CLIK!
CLIK!
DOOM ALWAYS HAS A FOOLPROOF MEANS OF ESCAPE AT HAND!

MY ARMOR MAY NO LONGER FULLY SERVE ME, THANKS TO THOSE SHARP-TOOTHED PESTS, BUT I AM NOT WITHOUT RESOURCES.
RRRUMMM

DOOM! DON'T BE A FOOL!
GOOD RIDDANCE!
UNTIL WE MEET AGAIN...
CLIK
CLIK
CLIK

CHRRT!
RRIIP
MY CLOAK!

YOU HAVE NOT HEARD THE LAST OF VICTOR VON DOOM! THIS INDIGNITY SHALL BE AVENGED!

THE DOOMSHIP IS SETTLING. AND THESE WOODS ARE INFESTED WITH VICIOUS RODENTS.
I MUST ESCAPE!
CUK CUK CUK

WATER AHEAD! MY ONLY CHANCE.
CUK CUK
CUK

VICTOR VON DOOM MUST NOT BE VANQUISHED IN THIS IGNOMINIOUS MANNER.
SPLOOSH!

CHRT!

HE SURE STIRRED UP A LOT OF MUD. I DON'T SEE HIM.
HIS BUILT-IN OXYGEN SUPPLY IS LIMITED.
ASSUMING IT'S STILL OPERABLE.

BLOP!
BLOP!

I DON'T LIKE THE LOOKS OF THAT. I'M GOING IN.
STAY PUT.
SPLASH
DON'T SWEAT IT. SQUIRRELS ARE GREAT SWIMMERS, BUT I'M NOT.

SEALS ARE WORKING. OXYGEN ON.
MY CHEST SEARCHLIGHT SHOULD CUT THROUGH THIS MURK.

THERE'S DOOM'S MASK...
AND THERE HE GOES--BURROWING INTO THE MUD LIKE A CLAM.
NOT SO FAST, DOOM. YOU AND I HAVE UNFINISHED BUSINESS.
NO GOOD! HIS ARMOR'S TOO SLIPPERY--SOME KIND OF SILICON COATING.
MUD. NOTHING BUT MUD.
GOT AWAY, HUH?
AFRAID SO.
SPLASH
SPLOOP!
GUK GUK
THANKS, MONKEY JOE. GOOD SQUIRREL.
CHIRP!
HERE. YOU SHOULD HAVE THIS.
MAYBE THERE ARE SOME NEAT SECRETS INSIDE.
THANKS.
I-I GUESS I KINDA MADE A MESS OF THINGS, HUH?
OH, I DON'T KNOW ABOUT THAT.
YOU MANAGED TO HAND DR. DOOM ONE OF THE MOST INGLORIOUS DEFEATS OF HIS CAREER.

STILL, I'M SO EMBARRASSED. I CAUSED YOU ALL KINDS OF PROBLEMS.

WE MAY NEVER KNOW WHAT HE WAS UP TO, BUT IT'S A CINCH WE SET DOOM'S PLANS BACK--AT LEAST FOR A WHILE.
ALL IN ALL, YOU DID PRETTY WELL.

DOES THAT MEAN YOU'LL TAKE ME ON AS YOUR PARTNER?

OUT OF THE QUESTION. SORRY.
WHAT AM I GOING TO DO? I'M NOT BIG ENOUGH TO GO SUPER HEROING ON MY OWN. AND I CAN'T GO BACK TO SCHOOL.
EVERYBODY CALLS ME "RODENT."

TAKE MY ADVICE. YOU'VE SEEN HOW DANGEROUS THIS BUSINESS IS. TAKE A FEW YEARS OFF. FINISH SCHOOL. GO TO COLLEGE.
IF YOU STILL WANT TO DO THIS AFTER YOU GRADUATE, LOOK ME UP.
YOU MEAN IT! YOU'LL GIVE ME A CHANCE THEN?

WHAT I MEANT WAS I'LL PUT IN A GOOD WORD FOR YOU WITH THE AVENGERS.
I'M NOT BIG ON CROWD SCENES. IF YOU DON'T MIND, I'LL KEEP LOOKING UNTIL I FIND SOMEONE WHO LIKES ME.

I LIKE YOU, HONEST. NO HARD FEELINGS?
WELL... OKAY. IT'S HARD TO STAY MAD AT A GUY IN GLEAMING ARMOR.
GOOD LUCK, SQUIRREL GIRL.

I DON'T NEED LUCK. I EAT NUTS.

"I DON'T NEED LUCK. I EAT NUTS."
THEY'RE NOT GOING TO BELIEVE THIS AT THE NEXT AVENGERS' MEETING.

THE END.

SQUIRREL GIRL... AGENT OF S.H.I.E.L.D.?!

HAPPY HOLIDAYS! SQUIRREL GIRL HERE. AND THIS IS MY GIRL-SQUIRREL, TIPPY-TOE!
WE JUST WANTED TO WELCOME YOU TO THE GLX-MAS SPECIAL AND WARN YOU ABOUT SOME 'A THE STUFF INSIDE...
...LIKE VIOLENCE, SUICIDE, AND AN INAPPROPRIATE USE OF THE WORD "FLOCK."
IF YOU THINK YOU MIGHT BE OFFENDED BY ANY OF THAT, MARVEL IS ALSO PUTTING OUT A PUNISHER X-MAS SPECIAL...SO, THERE YOU GO.
NOW SOME OF YOU MIGHT BE WONDERING WHY WE'RE NOT IN OUR COOL LEATHER COSTUMES FROM THE END OF OUR LAST ADVENTURE...
WELL, IT TURNS OUT THEY WERE ALL DESIGNED BY OUR ARCH-NEMESIS, LEATHER BOY, SO WE DECIDED NOT TO--
SQUIRREL GIRL?
SORRY TO INTERRUPT.
HI, DOORMAN. WHAT'S UP?
WE'RE ALMOST READY FOR THE PARTY, BUT WE NEED SOMEONE TO RUN DOWN TO THE STORE AND PICK UP EGGNOG AND TOILET PAPER.
NO PROBLEMO. WE'RE ON IT!
Chrrt
WHY, YES. IT IS A PRETTY SCARF. FLATMAN KNITTED IT UP FOR ME. WASN'T THAT NICE OF HIM?
NOW COME ALONG, GIRL! WE'RE ON AN IMPORTANT GLX MISSION!
TO THE SQUIRREL-A-GIG!

DECEMBER 24TH, 4:33 P.M. THE SKY ABOVE MILWAUKEE...
HOLD ON, GIRL. ARMS AND TAILS INSIDE.
WOWEE!
WE SURE ARE LUCKY BIG BERTHA WAS OUR SECRET SANTA! SHE GIVES THE BEST PRESENTS!
SQUIRREL GIRL IN "EGGNOG, TOILET PAPER, & PEACE ON EARTH"
Cuk cuk.
WHAT? YOU'RE HER SECRET SANTA? WELL, I HOPE YOU GOT HER SOMETHING GOOD!
Squee.
NO, I TRUST YOU. HEY, WHAT'S THAT OVER BY LAKE MICHIGAN?
BUNCH 'A GUYS SHOOTIN' LASERS AT EACH OTHER! AND ON THE DAY BEFORE CHRISTMAS!
BETTER GET DOWN THERE AND SEE WHAT THAT'S ALL ABOUT.
COMMANDER DUGAN! LOOK! SQUIRREL GIRL'S JUST SHOWN UP!
THANK GOD!

SQUIRREL GIRL! AM I EVER GLAD TO SEE YOU! I'M--
DUM DUM DUGAN, SECOND IN COMMAND OF S.H.I.E.L.D.
WHA--? HOW IN BLAZES DIDJA KNOW--
I'VE GOT ALL OF THE IRON MAN VS. SERIES BATTLE CARDS. DID YOU KNOW YOU HAVE A DEFENSE STAT OF 8?
NO, I DIDN'T.
MINE'S 6.
UM. WE COULD REALLY USE YOUR HELP HERE, MISSY.
A.I.M. AGENTS UNCOVERED A BASE AT THE BOTTOM OF THIS LAKE, AND THEY'RE RAIDIN' IT OF ALL ITS TECHNOLOGY!
BUT THAT WAS MAELSTROM'S BASE! AND HE HAD STUFF IN THERE THAT COULD DESTROY THE UNIVERSE!
WE'VE GOT TO STOP 'EM!
THEY'RE NOT WHO I'M WORRIED ABOUT, SISTER...
"...IT'S HIM, THEIR BOSS, THE EVER-MALEVOLENT MODOK!"
PITIFUL MINI-BRAINS! COWER BEFORE ME!

HMM... BATTLE CHAIR. MENTAL BLASTS. GIANT HEAD. YUP, THIS GUY'S IN THE BIG LEAGUES ALL RIGHT!
MODOK
COMMANDER DUGAN, CALL YOUR MEN BACK AND GIVE US A ROUND OF SUPPRESSING FIRE!
MY PARTNER AND I HAVE THIS ONE!
C'MON, TIPPY-TOE! WE'RE GOIN' OVER THE TOP!
YOU HEARD 'ER, BOYS!
ALL RIGHT, GIRL! ONE FUZZBALL SPECIAL, COMING UP!
ALLEY-OOP!
HSSS!
AHH! NOT THE FACE!

CURSES! ARMS TOO TINY! HEAD TOO BIG!
GET IT OFF! EXTEND ALL WEAPONS!
OH YEAH?
WHY DON'TCHA KEEP THOSE AIMED ON ME?
THE GIRL WITH SQUIRREL-AGILITY!
IMPOSSIBLE!
MISTER, I DON'T KNOW THE MEANING OF THE WORD!
WELL, ACTUALLY I DO. IT'S NOT LIKE I'M STUPID OR ANYTHING.
I JUST DON'T CHOOSE TO USE IT IN MY PERSONAL LEXICON. IT'S VERY DISEMPOWERING.
Chrtt.
WHAT? YOU FOUND A WAY IN? THAT'S A GREAT IDEA. GO FOR IT, GIRL!

AND I'LL SEE HOW MO' LIKES IT...
...WHEN I MASH SOME NUTS INTO HIS EXPOSED CIRCUITS!
STOP THAT! THOSE ARE DELICATE FIRING MECHANISMS! YOU COULD KILL US ALL!
CHUK CHUK
NO! INTERNAL POWER SHUTTING DOWN!
BATTLE CHAIR OFF-LINE! LIFE SUPPORT FAILING!
COLOSTOMY BAG LEAKING INTO BACKUP MEMORY!
WE SURRENDER! MEN, STAND DOWN! NOW!
THAT WAS SOME GRADE-A FIELD WORK, SQUIRREL GIRL!
AND TIPPY-TOE!
OF COURSE. LOOK, I WANNA SHOW YOU SUMTHIN'. WITH OUR TOP SECRET S.H.I.E.L.D. SATELLITES...
...WE BEEN KEEPIN' AN EYE ON YOU FER SOME TIME NOW, WATCHIN' YA TAKE DOWN SOME 'A THE WORLD'S BIGGEST THREATS!

MANDARIN
DOCTOR DOOM
GIGANTO
MAGNIFICATION X100
HECK, GIRLIE, WE THINK YOU'RE THE BEST SUPERHUMAN COMBATANT WE'VE EVER SEEN! AND, WELL, WE WUZ WONDERIN'...
...IF YOU'D LET US DEPUTIZE YA--AS A FULL-FLEDGED AGENT OF S.H.I.E.L.D.!
GOLLY! THANKS AN' ALL, MR. DUGAN. BUT I'M AFRAID I'M GONNA HAVE TO SAY NO. SEE...
"...I ALREADY BELONG TO A TEAM, AND A REAL SWELL ONE AT THAT."
HEY, GUYS! ANYTHING HAPPEN WHILE WE WERE OUT?
NAH. WHAT ABOUT YOU?
THE USUAL.
GOT THE EGGNOG?
YUP.
WHAT ABOUT THE TOILET PAPER?
D'OH! BE RIGHT BACK.

A FEW MINUTES LATER...
SO WHY DIDN'T YOU REMIND ME?
Squee!
WHAT? A SPACESHIP? WHERE?
OH MY! LOOK, TIPPY-TOE! SOMETHING'S COMING OUT OF IT!
YES! ONCE I, THANOS, HAVE CHARGED THE PYRAMATRIX WITH THE LIFE FORCE OF EVERYONE ON EARTH...
...THE UNIVERSE SHALL BE MINE FOR THE TAKING!
OH YEAH?
NOT IF I CAN HELP IT!
TIPPY-TOE SAYS:
Here we go again!
THE END...?

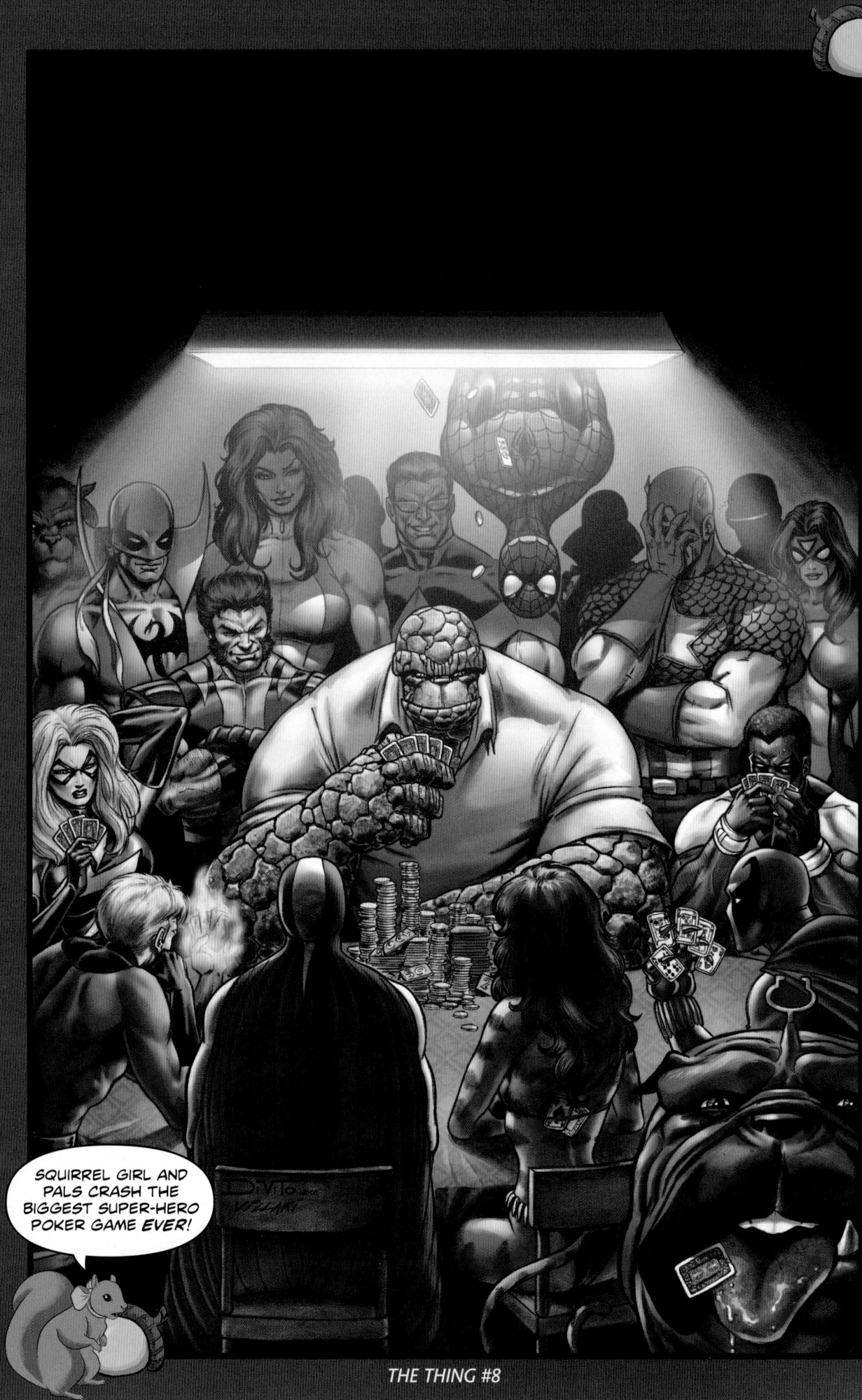
SQUIRREL GIRL AND PALS CRASH THE BIGGEST SUPER-HERO POKER GAME EVER!

THE THING #8

SATURDAY NIGHT...
READ 'EM AND WEEP, CHUMP. TWO PAIR, KINGS HIGH!
AND ONCE AGAIN I TAKE YOU TO THE CLEANERS! HA!
NOT SO FAST, CONSTRICTOR!
FOR IT APPEARS THE FATES FAVOR ME THIS NIGHT!
BEHOLD! THREE OF A KIND!
HA! HA! HA!
AND SO, AFTER MANY A TRAVAIL, DOES THE MIGHTY HERCULES FIND HIS FORTUNE RESTORED!
THIS CAN'T BE HAPPENING...
GUYS, COME ON. NO MORE A' THESE HIGH-STAKES SIDE-POTS, OKAY?
THAT'S NOT WHAT THIS'S ALL ABOUT.

LAST HAND
DAN SLOTT STORY
KIERON DWYER ARTIST
LAURA VILLARI COLORS
DAVE LANPHEAR LETTERS
SCHMIDT, LAZER & SITTERSON ASSISTANT EDITORS
TOM BREVOORT EDITOR
JOE QUESADA EDITOR IN CHIEF
DAN BUCKLEY PUBLISHER
'CAUSE TONIGHT, WE'RE JUST HERE TO HAVE SOME FUN!
SOME TURNOUT, HUH? USUALLY WE ONLY GOT A COUPLE SEATS AT ONE A' MY GAMES. BUT CONSIDERIN' THIS'S MY BIG DAY, I DECIDED TO PULL OUT ALL THE STOPS AND HOLD...
...THE FIRST-EVER SUPER HERO POKER TOURNAMENT! YEAH, THAT'S RIGHT. ALL THREE FLOORS A' MY SWANKY PENTHOUSE APARTMENT ARE PACKED WITH EVERY SUPER GUY AN' GAL YOU CAN THINK OF...
SORRY I'M LATE. WHAT'D I MISS?
TWO SUPER-VILLAIN ATTACKS, AN INCURSION FROM EARTH-A...
...AND WE HAD TO SEND OUT FOR MORE PIZZA.
HEY, NO DOUBLE-DIPPING!
SO, REED, I DON'T SEE YOUR WIFE ANYWHERE. SHE WOULDN'T BE...?
WALKING AROUND INVISIBLE? PEEKING AT YOUR CARDS?
SCOTT, PLEASE. WE'RE SUPER HEROES.
SO?
FOLD. HE'S GOT A STRAIGHT.

OLD SHIPWRE
IPA
...THOUGHT YOU HAD A NEW COSTUME?
WANNA SEE IT? IT'LL COST YOU TWENTY BUCKS.

...OF COURSE THAT DON'T MEAN IT AIN'T INVITATION-ONLY.
HEY, TRUE BELIEVERS! TIME TO GET THIS PARTY STARTED! 'CAUSE HERE COMES THE GLX!
THE WHO?
THE GLX. THAT'S US. WE'RE THE GREAT LAKES X-MEN!
X-MEN? I DON'T THINK SO.
SNAP
THINK AGAIN.
THINK AGAIN...
UM...
ER...
UH...
I KNOW. WE'RE THE GLD!
THE GREAT LAKES DEFENDERS!
KRAM
NO, YOU'RE NOT.
MR. I?
NO, WE'RE NOT. WE'RE... WE'RE...
I DON'T KNOW WHO WE ARE.
WELL WHOEVER YOU ARE, YOU'RE NOT ON THE LIST. SO WHY DON'T YOU TURN AROUND AND--
EASY, LUKE...

...LOOKS LIKE THOSE GUYS ARE HERE WITH SQUIRREL GIRL. I TOLD HER SHE COULD COME.
HEY, S.G.! TELL YER FRIENDS TO PULL UP A SEAT WHEREVER THEY WANT.

SQUIRREL GIRL, HUH? SO HOW DO YOU KNOW THE THING?
OH, MR. GRIMM AND I? WE JUST MET THE OTHER DAY.
GUESS YOU COULD SAY WE HAD ONE OF THOSE SUPER HERO TEAM-UPS YOU KEEP HEARING ABOUT.
LET'S SEE...

"...IT ALL STARTED WHILE I WAS LOOKING UP SOME OLD FRIENDS IN CENTRAL PARK..."
HEY, GUYS. MISS ME? THIS IS MY NEW PARTNER, TIPPY-TOE. SHE'S FROM MILWAUKEE.
TIPPY-TOE, SAY 'HI' TO THE GANG. TIPPY-TOE?
Chrt!

WHAT'S THAT, TIPPY-TOE? DANGER?!
QUICK, EVERYBODY! SCAMPER!
YOW! I'LL BE FEELIN' THAT ONE TOMORROW!
RUMF

WOWEE! I KNOW YOU! YOU'RE THE THING!
YOU'RE ON MY LUNCHBOX!
ARE YOU IN THE MIDDLE OF SOME BIG ADVENTURE? CAN I PITCH IN?
WHAT? NO! NOW GET OUTTA HERE-- WHOEVER YA ARE!

I'M SQUIRREL GIRL. LET ME HELP.
I CAN TALK TO SQUIRRELS, AND I'VE GOT SQUIRREL AGILITY. AND NUTS.
NUTS IS RIGHT, SISTER! 'CAUSE NONE A' THAT IS GONNA DO SQUAT AGAINST HIM!
TOOM
HE'S THE BI-BEAST! ONE A' THE HULK'S BADDIES!
AND SINCE OL' JADE JAWS AIN'T AROUND, I'M ALL THAT'S STANDIN' IN HIS WAY!
YOU?! HA! MY SKULL-BROTHER AND I ARE TWICE YOUR SIZE! TWICE AS STRONG! THE ULTIMATE TWO-IN-ONE FOE!
WE HAVE TWO SETS OF EYES FOR TWICE THE VISION!
TWO BRAINS FOR TWICE THE SMARTS!
AND TWO NOSES!
FOR TWICE THE... SMELLING.

WHAT? I'M BEING SERIOUS. HE'S GOT--
KID, I'M NOT GONNA TELL YA AGAIN. BEAT IT! JUST STICK TA YER SQUIRRELS, OKAY?!
OKAY.
YOU HEARD 'IM, FELLAS. WE'RE GONNA NEED ALL YOUR HELP ON THIS ONE!
HERE'S THE PLAN... CUKK CUKK CHRT CHRT SQUEE!
CUKK
CHRT
CUKK
MEN
SQUEE
CHRT
ONCE YOU ARE GONE, MY SKULL-BROTHER AND I SHALL DESTROY YOUR HUMAN SOCIETY!
YES! IN THE NAME OF OUR MAKERS, WE SHALL REDUCE YOUR WORLD TO ONE BIG PILE OF...OF...
KTAM
GNFF!
SNIFF SNIFF...UGH! DO YOU SMELL THAT?
EW! WHERE IS THAT COMING FROM?
DON'T LOOK AT ME!

SORRY, GUYS. THAT'S MY FAULT. I HAD MY SQUIRREL-FRIENDS GATHER UP...
...THE STINKIEST, SMELLIEST GARBAGE IN ALL OF CENTRAL PARK.
ECH! MAYGIT STOP!
AW GEEZ! WHY'B YOU GO AM DO DAT FOR?!
WELL, HE HAS TWO HAMBS AM TWO NOSES. YOU HAB TWO HAMBS AM ONE NOSE.
SO NOW, YOU'B GOT ONE OBER HIMB!
OR IM UBBER WURBS...
...IT'S CLOBBERIM' TIBE!
WAK
YA DIB GOOB DERE, KIB!
YEAH, GUESS YOU'B SAY...
...WE WUM BY A NOSE!
YOU WHAT?
SHE SAID WE "WON BY A NOSE."
C'MON, CAROL. THAT'S FREAKIN' ADORABLE.
BEN, THE ONLY THING THAT STINKS MORE THAN THAT STORY...
...IS THIS HAND. THAT'S IT. I'M OUT.

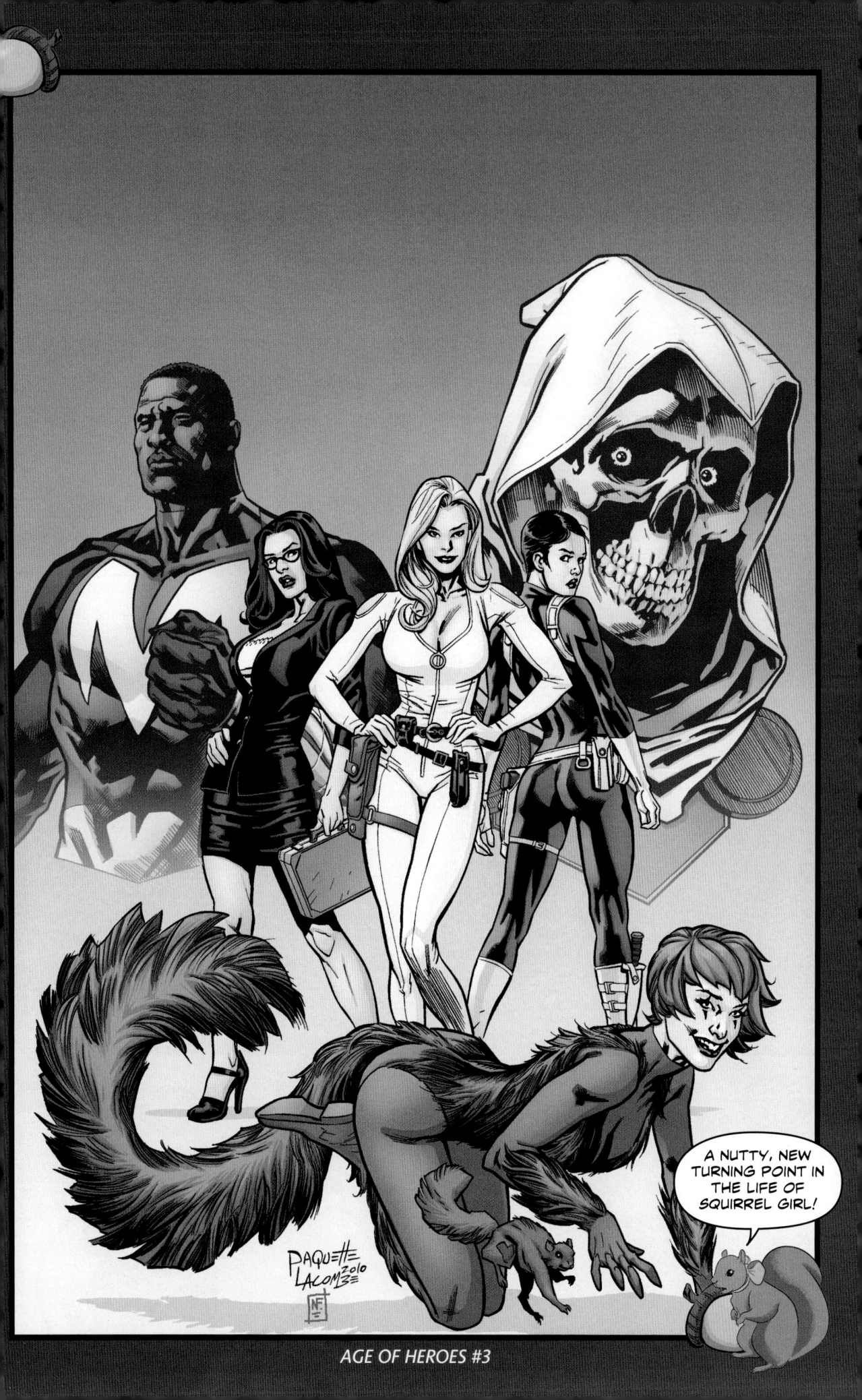

AGE OF HEROES #3

SQUIRREL GIRL IN "NUTS TO THIS!"

A SLOTT/TEMPLETON/MAESE/LANPHEAR JAM

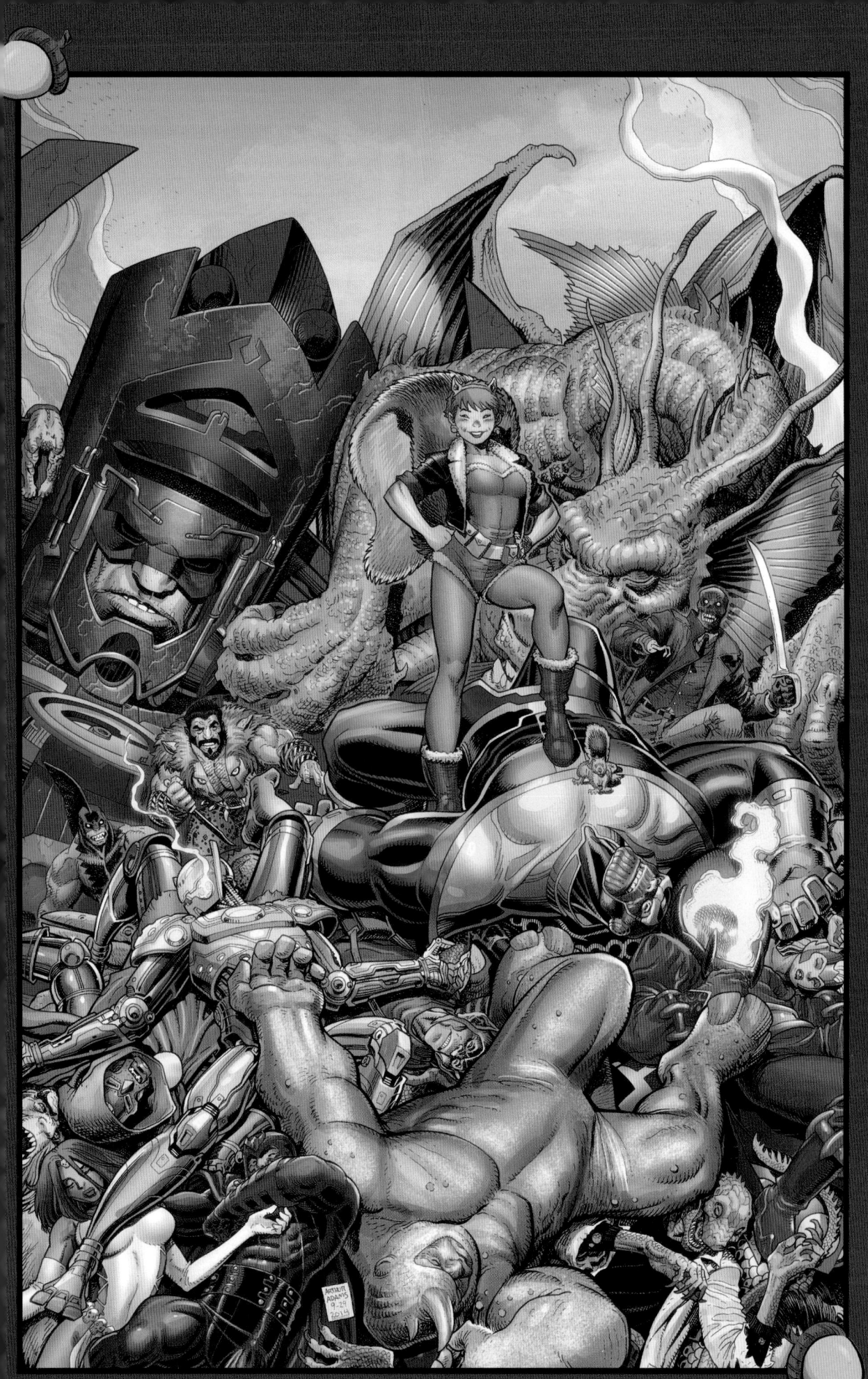

ISSUE #1 VARIANT COVER BY **ARTHUR ADAMS** & **PAUL MOUNTS**

Squirrel Girl is saying "EATS," but what could she be eating? If only there were also a reprinting of issue #2 whose cover clarified this matter in some way!

Oh, Squirrel Girl is eating nuts! Okay, that makes sense. That's really appropriate actually.

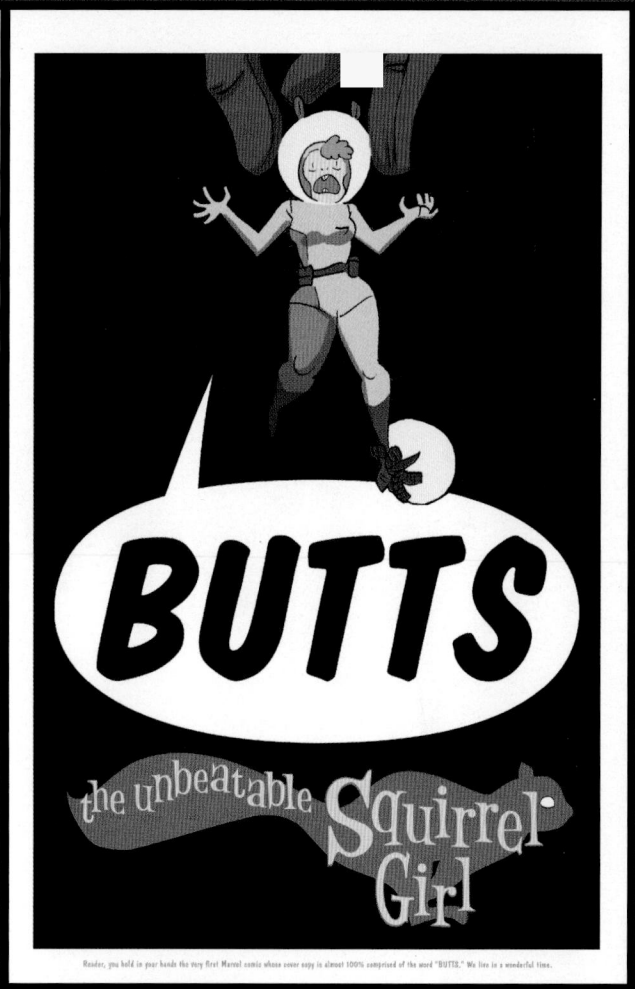

TOP ROW, FROM LEFT: ISSUE #1 3RD-PRINTING VARIANT COVER, ISSUE #2 3RD-PRINTING VARIANT COVER, ISSUE #3 2ND-PRINTING VARIANT COVER, ISSUE #4 2ND-PRINTING VARIANT COVER
RIGHT: ISSUE #5 2ND-PRINTING VARIANT COVER

ISSUE #1 VARIANT COVER BY **SKOTTIE YOUNG**

ISSUE #2 VARIANT COVER BY **JOE QUINONES**

ISSUE #3 VARIANT COVER BY **JILL THOMPSON**

ISSUE #3 VARIANT COVER BY **GURIHIRU**

THE END!
(FOR NOW...)